Title: Transforming Business for Good
Subtitle: A Comprehensive Guide to Innovation,
Ethics, and Data Analysis

Series: Understanding Money:
Finance and Economics Simplified
Author: Serenity Tanner

Table of Contents

Introduction
Purpose of the book

The purpose of this book is to provide readers with a comprehensive understanding of finance and economics, with a focus on the various financial parameters and formulas that are used to measure economic performance, analyze financial markets, and make investment decisions. By explaining these parameters and formulas in detail, the book aims to demystify the complex world of finance and economics and make it accessible to a wider audience.

The book is designed to be a useful resource for students, professionals, and anyone who wants to gain a better understanding of finance and economics. Whether you are a beginner who is just starting to learn about these subjects, or an experienced professional who wants to deepen your knowledge, this book will provide you with a solid foundation in the key concepts and principles of finance and economics.

The book is divided into nine chapters, each of which covers a different aspect of finance and economics. The first chapter provides an overview of macroeconomics, which is the study of the economy as a whole. This includes topics such as GDP, inflation, and unemployment, as well as the policies that governments use to manage the economy.

The second chapter focuses on microeconomics, which is the study of how individuals and firms make decisions about production, consumption, and pricing. This includes topics such as supply and demand, market structures, and pricing strategies.

The third chapter covers financial statements, which are the primary means by which companies communicate their financial performance to investors and other stakeholders. This includes topics such as the balance sheet, income statement, and statement of cash flows, as well as the various financial ratios that are used to analyze a company's financial health.

The fourth chapter is dedicated to investment analysis, which is the process of evaluating securities such as stocks, bonds, and mutual funds in order to make informed investment decisions. This includes topics such as risk and return, portfolio diversification, and asset allocation.

The fifth chapter covers financial markets, which are the mechanisms by which buyers and sellers of financial assets come together to trade. This includes topics such as the stock market, bond market, and foreign exchange market, as well as the various types of financial instruments that are traded in these markets.

The sixth chapter focuses on international finance, which is the study of the flow of money between countries. This includes topics such as exchange rates, balance of payments, and international trade.

The seventh chapter covers behavioral finance, which is the study of how psychology and emotions can affect financial decision-making. This includes topics such as biases, heuristics, and the role of emotions in investing.

The eighth chapter is dedicated to digital assets and blockchain technology, which are rapidly evolving areas of finance that have the potential to disrupt traditional financial systems. This includes topics such as cryptocurrencies, initial coin offerings, and smart contracts.

The ninth and final chapter presents case studies that apply the concepts and principles covered in the previous chapters to real-world situations. These case studies illustrate how finance and economics can be used to analyze and understand a wide range of economic and financial phenomena, from the global financial crisis to the rise of e-commerce.

Overall, this book aims to provide readers with a deep understanding of finance and economics, and to equip them with the tools and knowledge they need to make informed decisions about their personal finances and investments. By explaining the key concepts and principles of finance and economics in a clear and accessible manner, the book aims to empower readers to take control of their financial lives and achieve their financial goals.

Brief history of economics

Economics is a field of study that dates back to ancient times. In fact, economic principles were discussed by ancient Greek philosophers such as Aristotle and Plato. However, the modern study of economics began during the 18th century, when scholars began to use scientific methods to understand the behavior of markets and economies.

One of the most influential economists of the 18th century was Adam Smith, who is considered by many to be the founder of modern economics. Smith's most famous work, "The Wealth of Nations," was published in 1776 and argued that a free market economy, guided by the invisible hand of self-interest, would lead to the most efficient allocation of resources.

Throughout the 19th and 20th centuries, economics continued to evolve as scholars developed new theories and methods of analysis. One important development was the rise of Keynesian economics, which argued that government intervention was necessary to stabilize the economy during times of recession or depression. Keynesian economics became particularly influential during the Great Depression of the 1930s.

In the post-World War II era, economics underwent another major transformation as scholars began to use mathematical and statistical methods to analyze economic phenomena. This led to the development of econometrics, which is the use of statistical techniques to test economic theories and hypotheses.

Since the 1970s, economics has become increasingly specialized, with scholars focusing on particular subfields such as finance, labor economics, international trade, and development economics. However, many of the key questions and debates in economics remain the same, such as how to achieve economic growth and development, how to allocate resources efficiently, and how to address issues of inequality and poverty.

In this book, we will explore the key concepts, theories, and methods of modern economics, with a focus on how they can be used to understand and analyze real-world economic issues. We will begin by discussing the principles of microeconomics and macroeconomics, and then move on to explore topics such as international trade, financial markets, and economic development. Through this exploration, we hope to provide readers with a deeper understanding of the fascinating and complex field of economics.

Importance of economics in society

Economics plays a vital role in society, influencing everything from government policy to individual decision-making. In this section, we will explore the importance of economics in society and how it affects our daily lives.

Firstly, economics provides a framework for understanding how society allocates scarce resources. Scarcity is a fundamental concept in economics, as it means that there are limited resources to meet unlimited wants and needs. By studying economics, we can learn how to make the most efficient use of these resources to satisfy our wants and needs.

Secondly, economics helps to inform government policy. For example, policymakers may use economic models and data to determine the best course of action to address issues such as inflation, unemployment, and economic growth. Economic theories and empirical evidence can also help to inform policy debates on issues such as taxation, social welfare, and environmental regulation.

Thirdly, economics plays a crucial role in business and finance. Business owners and managers use economic analysis to make decisions about pricing, production, and investment. Financial markets, such as the stock market and bond market, are also heavily influenced by economic factors such as interest rates, inflation, and economic growth.

Fourthly, economics provides insights into international trade and globalization. By studying international economics, we can understand the benefits and challenges of international trade and how it can affect both developed and developing countries.

Finally, economics is important for individual decision-making. By understanding basic economic principles such as opportunity cost and marginal analysis, individuals can make more informed decisions about how to allocate their time and resources.

In summary, economics is a vital field of study that influences many aspects of our lives. By studying economics, we can gain a better understanding of how society allocates scarce resources, inform government policy, make better business and financial decisions, and understand the complexities of international trade and globalization.

Chapter 1: Macroeconomics
Principles of macroeconomics

Macroeconomics is the study of the economy as a whole, focusing on the performance and behavior of national economies. In this section, we will explore the principles of macroeconomics, which provide a framework for understanding the broader economic issues that affect society.

One of the central principles of macroeconomics is the concept of gross domestic product (GDP), which measures the total value of goods and services produced within a country's borders during a given period. GDP is an important indicator of economic performance and is used to track changes in the overall level of economic activity.

Another key principle of macroeconomics is the concept of inflation, which is the sustained increase in the general level of prices over time. Inflation is measured by the consumer price index (CPI), which tracks the price changes of a basket of goods and services consumed by households. Understanding inflation is important as it can affect the purchasing power of consumers, the competitiveness of businesses, and the stability of financial markets.

Unemployment is another crucial topic in macroeconomics. It refers to the percentage of the labor force that is unemployed but actively seeking employment. The level of unemployment is closely monitored by policymakers as it can indicate the overall health of the economy and can be affected by factors such as government policies, technological changes, and global economic conditions.

Another important principle of macroeconomics is fiscal policy, which involves the use of government spending and taxation to influence the overall level of economic activity. For example, during periods of recession, governments may increase spending or cut taxes to stimulate economic growth. Conversely, during periods of inflation, governments may reduce spending or increase taxes to cool down the economy.

Finally, monetary policy is another key area of macroeconomics, which involves the use of central bank policies to influence the level of economic activity. One of the main tools of monetary policy is the manipulation of interest rates, which can affect borrowing and lending behavior, investment decisions, and the overall level of economic activity.

In summary, the principles of macroeconomics provide a framework for understanding the broader economic issues that affect society. These principles include gross domestic product, inflation, unemployment, fiscal policy, and monetary policy, and are crucial for policymakers, businesses, and individuals to make informed decisions about economic issues.

Gross Domestic Product (GDP)

Gross Domestic Product (GDP) is one of the most widely used measures of economic activity, both domestically and internationally. It is a measure of the total value of all goods and services produced within a country's borders during a specific time period, typically a year. GDP is an important metric for policymakers, investors, and businesses, as it provides insight into the health and performance of a country's economy.

One of the primary uses of GDP is to measure the economic growth of a country over time. When GDP increases, it is generally seen as a positive sign that the economy is growing, whereas a decrease in GDP is typically seen as a sign of economic contraction. Additionally, GDP can be broken down into different components, such as consumer spending, government spending, investment, and net exports, which can provide additional insights into the factors driving economic growth.

There are different methods for calculating GDP, including the expenditure approach, income approach, and production approach. The expenditure approach is the most commonly used method and adds up all of the spending on goods and services within a country. The income approach looks at the income earned by households and businesses in the economy, while the production approach adds up the value of all goods and services produced.

It is important to note that GDP has limitations as a measure of economic activity. For example, it does not take into account non-market activities, such as household work or volunteer work, and does not account for the distribution of income within a country. Additionally, it does not account for environmental or social factors that may impact the well-being of a country's citizens.

Overall, GDP is a key metric for understanding the health and performance of a country's economy. Policymakers, investors, and businesses rely on this measure to make informed decisions about economic policy, investment strategies, and market opportunities.

Inflation

Inflation refers to the sustained increase in the general price level of goods and services in an economy over a certain period of time. It is measured by the Consumer Price Index (CPI), which tracks changes in the prices of a basket of goods and services commonly consumed by households. Inflation can have a significant impact on the economy and individuals' lives, including their purchasing power, income, and savings.

There are several types of inflation, including demand-pull inflation, cost-push inflation, and hyperinflation. Demand-pull inflation occurs when the demand for goods and services exceeds the supply, causing prices to rise. This type of inflation is often associated with periods of economic growth when consumers have more money to spend. Cost-push inflation occurs when the cost of production increases, leading to higher prices for goods and services. This type of inflation is often caused by factors such as an increase in the cost of raw materials or labor. Hyperinflation is a rapid and excessive increase in prices, often exceeding 50% per month, and is usually associated with political instability and a loss of confidence in a country's currency.

Inflation can have both positive and negative effects on the economy. In the short term, moderate inflation can stimulate economic growth by encouraging consumer spending and business investment. However, high or unpredictable inflation can have negative effects, including reducing the purchasing power of consumers, increasing the cost of borrowing, and causing uncertainty in the market.

Central banks often use monetary policy tools such as adjusting interest rates and implementing quantitative easing to control inflation. Governments can also implement fiscal policy measures such as increasing taxes or reducing spending to manage inflation.

Understanding inflation and its impact on the economy is important for individuals, businesses, and policymakers. By monitoring inflation trends, individuals can make informed decisions about their investments and savings, while businesses and policymakers can implement strategies to maintain a stable and healthy economy.

Unemployment

Unemployment is a crucial economic indicator that measures the percentage of the workforce that is without work but actively seeking employment. It is an essential metric in macroeconomics as it provides insight into the state of the labor market and the overall health of the economy. In this section, we will discuss the different types of unemployment and their causes, as well as their impacts on the economy and society.

Types of Unemployment:

1. Frictional Unemployment: This type of unemployment is caused by workers transitioning between jobs or entering the workforce. It is a natural part of the labor market and tends to be short-term.

2. Structural Unemployment: This type of unemployment is caused by changes in the structure of the economy. For example, advances in technology may render certain jobs obsolete, resulting in unemployment for workers in those industries.

3. Cyclical Unemployment: This type of unemployment is caused by downturns in the business cycle. When the economy is in a recession, businesses may cut jobs to save costs, resulting in higher unemployment.

Causes of Unemployment:

1. Lack of Demand for Labor: When businesses are not hiring due to a lack of demand for their goods and services, there is less demand for labor.

2. Technological Advances: As mentioned earlier, advances in technology can make certain jobs obsolete, resulting in unemployment.

3. Economic Recession: During an economic recession, businesses may cut jobs to save costs, resulting in higher unemployment.

Impacts of Unemployment:

1. Economic Impact: Unemployment can have a significant impact on the economy, as it reduces consumer spending, leading to a decrease in demand for goods and services, which can cause further unemployment.

2. Social Impact: Unemployment can also have a social impact, as it can lead to increased crime rates, substance abuse, and mental health issues.

3. Political Impact: High unemployment rates can also have political implications, as it can lead to dissatisfaction with the government and calls for policy changes.

In conclusion, unemployment is a critical economic indicator that provides insight into the state of the labor market and the overall health of the economy. By understanding the different types and causes of unemployment, as well as its impacts on society, policymakers can develop strategies to reduce unemployment rates and improve economic stability.

Business cycle

The business cycle refers to the fluctuations in economic activity that occur over a period of time. These fluctuations are often characterized by the expansion and contraction of the economy. The business cycle is an important concept in macroeconomics because it helps economists to understand the behavior of the economy as a whole.

The business cycle has four phases: expansion, peak, contraction, and trough. During the expansion phase, the economy is growing, employment is increasing, and inflation is typically rising. At the peak of the business cycle, the economy has reached its maximum level of growth, and is often followed by a contraction phase.

During the contraction phase, economic activity slows down, and unemployment typically rises. Inflation may also slow down or even turn into deflation. At the trough of the business cycle, the economy has reached its lowest level of activity, and is often followed by the beginning of a new expansion phase.

One of the key drivers of the business cycle is changes in aggregate demand. Aggregate demand refers to the total demand for goods and services in an economy. When aggregate demand is high, businesses may expand to meet the demand, and this can lead to an expansion phase. Conversely, when aggregate demand falls, businesses may cut back on production and employment, leading to a contraction phase.

Other factors that can impact the business cycle include changes in monetary policy, such as changes in interest rates, and changes in fiscal policy, such as changes in government spending or taxation. Additionally, external shocks such as changes in international trade or unexpected natural disasters can also impact the business cycle.

Understanding the business cycle is important for both policymakers and investors. For policymakers, it can help them to make informed decisions about monetary and fiscal policy. For investors, it can help them to identify opportunities for investment and to manage their risk exposure.

In summary, the business cycle is an important concept in macroeconomics that helps us to understand the fluctuations in economic activity that occur over time. By understanding the different phases of the business cycle and the factors that drive it, we can make better decisions about policy and investment.

Fiscal policy

Fiscal policy refers to the government's use of taxation and spending to influence the economy. The goal of fiscal policy is to stabilize the economy by achieving full employment, price stability, and economic growth. In this section, we will discuss the principles of fiscal policy, the tools that the government can use to implement fiscal policy, and the effectiveness of fiscal policy.

Principles of Fiscal Policy

Fiscal policy is based on several principles. One of the most important principles is the concept of budget balance. The government's budget balance is the difference between its revenues and expenditures. If the government spends more than it earns in revenues, it runs a budget deficit, which can lead to an increase in public debt. On the other hand, if the government earns more than it spends, it runs a budget surplus, which can be used to reduce public debt.

Another important principle of fiscal policy is the concept of automatic stabilizers. Automatic stabilizers are government programs that automatically increase spending or decrease taxes during a recession and decrease spending or increase taxes during an expansion. These programs include unemployment insurance, welfare programs, and progressive income taxes. Automatic stabilizers help to stabilize the economy by providing a cushion during a downturn and reducing the risk of inflation during an expansion.

Tools of Fiscal Policy

The government has two main tools that it can use to implement fiscal policy: taxation and government spending. The government can increase or decrease taxes to influence the level of economic activity. If the government wants to increase economic activity, it can decrease taxes, which will increase disposable income and consumer spending. On the other hand, if the government wants to reduce economic activity, it can increase taxes, which will decrease disposable income and consumer spending.

Government spending is another tool that the government can use to implement fiscal policy. The government can increase or decrease its spending on goods and services to influence the level of economic activity. If the government wants to increase economic activity, it can increase its spending on goods and services, which will create jobs and stimulate economic growth. On the other hand, if the government wants to reduce economic activity, it can decrease its spending on goods and services, which will reduce economic growth and job creation.

Effectiveness of Fiscal Policy

The effectiveness of fiscal policy depends on several factors, including the state of the economy, the size of the multiplier effect, and the time lags involved in implementing fiscal policy. The multiplier effect is the concept that a change in government spending or taxes can have a larger impact on the economy than the initial change. For example, if the government increases spending by $100 million, the overall impact on the economy may be much larger than $100 million due to the multiplier effect.

The time lags involved in implementing fiscal policy can also affect its effectiveness. There are two types of time lags: recognition lags and implementation lags. Recognition lags are the time it takes for policymakers to recognize that the economy is in a recession or expansion. Implementation lags are the time it takes for policymakers to implement fiscal policy once they have recognized the need for it. These time lags can reduce the effectiveness of fiscal policy, as the economy may have already moved in the opposite direction by the time the policy is implemented.

In conclusion, fiscal policy is an important tool that the government can use to stabilize the economy. By using taxation and government spending, the government can influence the level of economic activity and achieve its macroeconomic goals. However, the effectiveness of fiscal policy depends on several factors, including the state of the economy, the size of the multiplier effect, and the time lags involved in implementing fiscal policy.

Chapter 2: Microeconomics
Principles of microeconomics

Microeconomics is the study of individual and firm behavior in the market. It is concerned with the decisions made by consumers, producers, and government agencies in allocating resources. In this section, we will discuss the principles of microeconomics and how they impact individuals and businesses.

One of the fundamental principles of microeconomics is the law of supply and demand. This law states that the price of a good or service is determined by the interaction of supply and demand. When the supply of a good or service is high and the demand is low, the price will be low. Conversely, when the supply is low and the demand is high, the price will be high.

Another important principle is the concept of elasticity. Elasticity measures the responsiveness of demand or supply to changes in price or income. If the demand for a good or service is highly elastic, it means that consumers are very sensitive to changes in price. On the other hand, if the demand is inelastic, consumers are less sensitive to price changes.

Microeconomics also deals with the concept of market structures, which refers to the level of competition in a particular market. There are four types of market structures: perfect competition, monopolistic competition, oligopoly, and monopoly. Each market structure has its own unique characteristics that affect the behavior of firms and the prices of goods and services.

In addition, microeconomics examines the role of government intervention in markets. Governments can regulate prices, impose taxes, and provide subsidies to influence the behavior of firms and consumers. This can impact the efficiency of markets and lead to unintended consequences.

Overall, understanding the principles of microeconomics is crucial for individuals and businesses to make informed decisions in the market. By analyzing the behavior of consumers, producers, and government agencies, microeconomics can provide insights into how markets function and how they can be improved.

Supply and demand

Supply and demand is one of the foundational concepts in microeconomics, which is concerned with the behavior of individual consumers and firms. In this chapter, we will explore the principles of supply and demand, how they interact to determine market prices, and how changes in supply and demand can affect market outcomes.

The law of demand states that, all else being equal, as the price of a good or service increases, the quantity demanded decreases. Conversely, as the price of a good or service decreases, the quantity demanded increases. This relationship between price and quantity demanded is represented by the downward-sloping demand curve.

On the other hand, the law of supply states that, all else being equal, as the price of a good or service increases, the quantity supplied increases. Conversely, as the price of a good or service decreases, the quantity supplied decreases. This relationship between price and quantity supplied is represented by the upward-sloping supply curve.

The intersection of the demand and supply curves determines the equilibrium price and quantity for a good or service. At this point, the quantity demanded equals the quantity supplied, and there is no excess supply or excess demand in the market.

Changes in supply and demand can shift the demand or supply curve, leading to a new equilibrium price and quantity.

For example, an increase in consumer income can shift the demand curve for a normal good to the right, leading to a higher equilibrium price and quantity. A decrease in the cost of production can shift the supply curve to the right, leading to a lower equilibrium price and higher quantity.

Understanding supply and demand is important for businesses, policymakers, and consumers alike. Businesses need to know how changes in supply and demand will affect their sales and profits. Policymakers use this information to design effective economic policies. Consumers can use their understanding of supply and demand to make informed decisions about what goods and services to buy, and at what prices.

Market structures

Market structures refer to the different types of markets in which goods and services are exchanged. These structures vary based on the number of buyers and sellers, the level of competition, the ease of entry and exit, and the degree of product differentiation.

There are four primary market structures: perfect competition, monopolistic competition, oligopoly, and monopoly.

1. Perfect Competition: Perfect competition is characterized by a large number of buyers and sellers who are price takers, meaning they have no influence on the price of the product. In this market structure, all firms produce homogeneous products, meaning they are identical in terms of quality and features. The market is free of any barriers to entry or exit, and firms earn only normal profits in the long run.

2. Monopolistic Competition: Monopolistic competition is similar to perfect competition in terms of the number of buyers and sellers, but firms produce differentiated products, meaning they are not identical. This product differentiation allows firms to have some control over the price of their products, but they are still price takers in the market. There are low barriers to entry and exit, and firms can earn economic profits in the short run, but only normal profits in the long run.

3. Oligopoly: Oligopoly refers to a market structure where a small number of large firms dominate the market.

These firms are interdependent, meaning their actions have an impact on each other's profits. Firms may produce homogeneous or differentiated products, and barriers to entry are high, which can create barriers to competition. The degree of competition can vary, and firms can earn economic profits in both the short and long run.

4. Monopoly: Monopoly is characterized by a single seller who dominates the market and has complete control over the price of the product. There are high barriers to entry, which prevent other firms from entering the market and competing. The monopolist can earn economic profits in the long run, and may use its market power to restrict output and charge higher prices.

Understanding market structures is important for businesses and policymakers because it affects the behavior of firms, the level of competition, and the welfare of consumers. It can also help in identifying market failures and developing policies to address them.

Consumer behavior

Consumer behavior is a crucial aspect of microeconomics that focuses on how individuals or households make decisions about purchasing goods and services. It examines the psychological, social, and economic factors that influence consumer choices. Understanding consumer behavior is essential for businesses and marketers to create effective marketing strategies and increase sales.

One of the key determinants of consumer behavior is the price of the product or service. Price elasticity of demand is used to measure the sensitivity of consumers to changes in price. For example, if a product's price increases, consumers may switch to a substitute or stop purchasing altogether. On the other hand, if the price decreases, consumers may purchase more of the product.

Another determinant of consumer behavior is income. As income increases, consumers tend to spend more on normal goods, which are goods that have a positive income elasticity of demand. In contrast, as income decreases, consumers may switch to inferior goods, which are goods that have a negative income elasticity of demand. For example, a consumer may switch from purchasing steak to ground beef if their income decreases.

Consumer behavior is also influenced by advertising and marketing efforts. Companies use advertising to create brand awareness and persuade consumers to purchase their products.

Advertising can be done through various channels, such as television, radio, social media, and billboards. In addition, companies use promotions and discounts to incentivize consumers to make purchases.

Social and psychological factors also play a significant role in consumer behavior. Social factors include cultural norms, family, and social class, which can influence what products consumers purchase. For example, a consumer from a wealthy family may purchase luxury goods to maintain their social status. Psychological factors include perception, motivation, and attitudes, which can influence how consumers perceive products and make purchasing decisions.

Finally, consumer behavior is also affected by the availability of information. With the advent of the internet, consumers have access to a wealth of information about products and services. Online reviews, social media, and comparison websites allow consumers to make more informed purchasing decisions. Companies need to take this into account when creating their marketing strategies and ensure that they provide accurate and useful information about their products.

In conclusion, understanding consumer behavior is critical for businesses to create effective marketing strategies and increase sales. It involves examining the various factors that influence consumer choices, such as price, income, advertising, social and psychological factors, and the availability of information. By understanding these factors, businesses can create products and services that meet the needs and desires of their target market.

Price elasticity

Price elasticity is a key concept in microeconomics that measures the responsiveness of consumers to changes in the price of a good or service. It refers to the percentage change in quantity demanded for a good or service in response to a 1% change in price. The concept of price elasticity is important for businesses and policymakers to understand as it helps in making pricing and production decisions, and also helps in analyzing the impact of taxes and subsidies.

The formula for price elasticity is:

Price elasticity of demand = (% change in quantity demanded) / (% change in price)

If the price elasticity of demand is greater than one, it means that the demand for the good or service is elastic, i.e., consumers are highly responsive to changes in price. In this case, a decrease in price would lead to a significant increase in quantity demanded, and vice versa.

On the other hand, if the price elasticity of demand is less than one, it means that the demand for the good or service is inelastic, i.e., consumers are not very responsive to changes in price. In this case, a decrease in price would lead to a relatively small increase in quantity demanded, and vice versa.

Price elasticity can be used to determine the optimal price for a product or service. For example, if a business has an elastic product, it can increase sales by lowering the price, while still maintaining a high profit margin. Conversely, if a business has an inelastic product, it can increase profits by raising the price, while still maintaining a similar level of sales.

Price elasticity can also help policymakers analyze the impact of taxes and subsidies on consumer behavior. For example, if a government imposes a tax on a good or service, the price of the good or service will increase, which will cause a decrease in quantity demanded. The extent of this decrease will depend on the price elasticity of the good or service. Similarly, if a government provides a subsidy, the price of the good or service will decrease, which will cause an increase in quantity demanded, again depending on the price elasticity.

In summary, price elasticity is a key concept in microeconomics that helps businesses and policymakers understand the responsiveness of consumers to changes in price. It provides valuable insights into pricing and production decisions, and also helps in analyzing the impact of taxes and subsidies on consumer behavior.

Game theory

Game theory is a branch of microeconomics that examines the behavior of individuals, firms, and governments in strategic situations where the outcome of one person's decision depends on the decisions made by others. It involves analyzing the choices made by players in a game, the incentives that drive those choices, and the resulting outcomes.

The concept of game theory can be applied to various areas of study, including economics, political science, psychology, and biology. It provides a framework for understanding how individuals and organizations interact with each other and make decisions in situations where the outcome depends on the actions of others.

In game theory, a game is a situation where two or more players make decisions that affect each other. Each player has a set of available strategies, and the outcome of the game depends on the strategies chosen by all players. The most well-known example of a game is the prisoner's dilemma, where two criminals are being interrogated separately and must decide whether to confess or remain silent. The outcome of the game depends on the choices made by both criminals.

Game theory has numerous applications in economics, including oligopoly theory, industrial organization, and public choice theory. In oligopoly theory, game theory is used to analyze the behavior of firms in markets where there are only a few dominant players. In industrial organization, game theory is used to analyze strategic interactions between firms, such as price wars or advertising campaigns. In public choice theory, game theory is used to analyze the behavior of politicians and voters in elections and other political contests.

One of the key concepts in game theory is the Nash equilibrium, named after the economist John Nash. A Nash equilibrium is a situation where each player's strategy is optimal given the strategies chosen by all other players. In other words, no player can improve their outcome by changing their strategy, given the strategies chosen by others.

Another important concept in game theory is the concept of dominant strategies. A dominant strategy is a strategy that is always optimal, regardless of the strategies chosen by other players. In some games, such as the prisoner's dilemma, there is no dominant strategy, and players must make strategic choices based on their expectations of what other players will do.

Game theory has been used to explain a wide range of phenomena, including the behavior of firms in markets, the effectiveness of deterrence strategies in international relations, and the evolution of cooperation in social networks. It has also been applied to numerous real-world situations, such as auctions, bargaining, and voting.

Overall, game theory is a powerful tool for understanding the behavior of individuals, firms, and governments in strategic situations. Its applications are numerous and diverse, making it a valuable tool for economists, political scientists, and other social scientists.

Chapter 3: Finance

Principles of finance

Finance is the study of money management, investments, and financial institutions. It is a critical component of any economy, and its principles are essential to understanding the financial world. In this chapter, we will explore the principles of finance and how they relate to personal finance, corporate finance, and investments.

Time Value of Money:

One of the fundamental principles of finance is the time value of money. It states that the value of money today is worth more than the same amount of money in the future due to inflation and the opportunity cost of using that money today. This principle is used to evaluate investment opportunities and to make financial decisions that will maximize wealth over time.

Risk and Return:

Another critical principle of finance is the relationship between risk and return. It is generally true that the higher the risk of an investment, the higher the potential return. This principle is used to evaluate the risk of investments and to make decisions about where to allocate funds.

Financial Markets:

Financial markets are an essential component of finance, and they play a critical role in the allocation of capital. They are the mechanisms through which savers and borrowers are connected and through which financial instruments are bought and sold. Financial markets can be categorized into two types: primary markets and secondary markets.

Capital Budgeting:

Capital budgeting is the process of evaluating long-term investment opportunities. This process involves analyzing the costs and benefits of potential investments and determining which investments are most likely to increase the value of the firm. Capital budgeting is essential for corporations, as it allows them to make strategic investment decisions that will maximize shareholder wealth.

Cost of Capital:

The cost of capital is the cost that a company incurs to raise capital for its operations. It includes the cost of equity, which is the return required by investors to invest in the company's stock, and the cost of debt, which is the interest rate required by lenders to lend money to the company. The cost of capital is a critical concept in corporate finance, as it is used to evaluate investment opportunities and to determine the appropriate mix of debt and equity financing.

Financial Statements:

Financial statements are reports that provide information about a company's financial performance and position. They include the income statement, balance sheet, and statement of cash flows. Financial statements are used by investors, analysts, and managers to evaluate the financial health of a company and to make decisions about investing, lending, and operating the company.

Conclusion:

The principles of finance are essential to understanding how money works in the modern economy. They are used by individuals, corporations, and governments to make decisions about investments, financing, and operations. The principles of finance covered in this chapter provide a foundation for understanding more complex financial concepts and tools.

Corporate finance

Corporate finance refers to the financial activities of corporations and the methods used to manage and raise capital. It is concerned with the financial decisions that businesses make, including investment decisions, financing decisions, and dividend decisions. The main goal of corporate finance is to maximize the value of the corporation to its shareholders.

One of the primary responsibilities of corporate finance is to manage a company's finances to ensure it can operate effectively and profitably. Corporate finance professionals use financial analysis tools to evaluate a company's financial health and identify areas for improvement. These professionals also analyze potential investments, financing options, and risk management strategies to make informed decisions about the company's future.

Corporate finance also involves the process of raising capital for a company. This can include issuing stocks or bonds, taking on debt through loans or credit lines, or pursuing alternative financing methods like crowdfunding or venture capital. These financing decisions are made with the goal of optimizing the company's capital structure, or the mix of debt and equity used to finance the company's operations.

Another important aspect of corporate finance is dividend policy. This refers to the decision-making process around how a company distributes profits to its shareholders. Corporate finance professionals evaluate the company's financial position and future growth prospects to determine the appropriate level of dividend payments. This decision must balance the needs of shareholders for income with the company's need for capital to reinvest in the business.

Corporate finance is an essential function of any successful business. It helps companies make informed financial decisions, manage their finances effectively, and raise capital to support growth and expansion. By maximizing the value of the corporation to its shareholders, corporate finance professionals play a crucial role in ensuring the long-term success of a company.

Investments, including digital assets and cryptocurrencies

Investments are one of the most important aspects of finance. It involves allocating resources in a manner that will generate a return in the future. Investments can be broadly classified into two categories: traditional investments and alternative investments. Traditional investments include stocks, bonds, and mutual funds, while alternative investments include real estate, commodities, hedge funds, private equity, and digital assets such as cryptocurrencies.

Digital assets, particularly cryptocurrencies, have become an increasingly popular investment option over the past decade. Cryptocurrencies are digital or virtual tokens that use cryptography for security and are often decentralized, meaning they are not controlled by any central authority. The most well-known cryptocurrency is Bitcoin, but there are thousands of other cryptocurrencies available for investment.

Investing in cryptocurrencies can be risky and requires careful consideration of various factors. The following are some of the key factors to consider when investing in digital assets:

1. Market volatility: Cryptocurrency markets are notoriously volatile, and prices can fluctuate rapidly. This can lead to significant gains but also significant losses. Investors should be prepared for market volatility and have a strategy in place to manage risk.

2. Security: Cryptocurrencies are stored in digital wallets, and these wallets can be vulnerable to hacking and cyber-attacks. Investors should take steps to ensure that their wallets are secure and protected.

3. Regulation: The regulatory landscape for cryptocurrencies is constantly evolving, and there is a lot of uncertainty surrounding how cryptocurrencies will be regulated in the future. Investors should stay informed about regulatory developments and the potential impact on their investments.

4. Liquidity: Cryptocurrency markets are still relatively small compared to traditional financial markets, and this can lead to liquidity issues. Investors may find it difficult to buy or sell large amounts of cryptocurrencies without affecting the market price.

5. Technology: Cryptocurrencies rely on complex technology, and investors should have a basic understanding of how this technology works. This includes understanding the concept of blockchain, which is the underlying technology that powers most cryptocurrencies.

Investing in cryptocurrencies is not suitable for everyone, and investors should carefully consider their financial goals and risk tolerance before investing. It is also important to note that cryptocurrencies are not backed by any government or financial institution and are not insured, which means that investors may lose all of their investment.

In addition to cryptocurrencies, there are other digital assets that investors may consider, such as digital art, virtual real estate, and non-fungible tokens (NFTs). These assets are also relatively new and can be difficult to value, making them a high-risk investment option.

Overall, while digital assets offer new investment opportunities, investors should be cautious and informed before investing in them. Understanding the risks and potential rewards of digital assets is essential for making informed investment decisions.

Personal finance

Personal finance refers to the management of an individual's finances. It is the practice of managing one's money, including saving, investing, budgeting, and managing debt. Personal finance is a critical aspect of an individual's life, as it affects their quality of life, financial stability, and future prospects. In this chapter, we will cover the principles of personal finance and the different aspects involved in managing one's finances.

1. Budgeting Budgeting is the foundation of personal finance. It is the process of creating a plan for how to spend and save money over a specific period. A budget can help an individual to manage their expenses and make informed financial decisions. In this section, we will discuss the importance of budgeting, how to create a budget, and the different types of budgets.

2. Saving Saving is the act of putting money aside for future use. Saving is an essential aspect of personal finance as it helps individuals to achieve their financial goals, such as buying a house, starting a business, or retiring comfortably. In this section, we will discuss the importance of saving, different types of savings accounts, and strategies for saving money.

3. Investing Investing is the act of using money to buy assets that are expected to increase in value over time. Investing is a critical aspect of personal finance as it can help individuals to build wealth and achieve their long-term

financial goals. In this section, we will discuss the different types of investments, such as stocks, bonds, mutual funds, and real estate, and the factors to consider when investing.

4. Managing debt Debt is money that an individual owes to another entity, such as a bank or credit card company. Managing debt is an essential aspect of personal finance as it can affect an individual's credit score and financial stability. In this section, we will discuss the different types of debt, such as credit card debt, student loans, and mortgages, and strategies for managing debt.

5. Retirement planning Retirement planning is the process of preparing for retirement by saving and investing for the future. Retirement planning is a critical aspect of personal finance as it helps individuals to achieve financial independence and maintain their standard of living in retirement. In this section, we will discuss the importance of retirement planning, different types of retirement accounts, and strategies for retirement planning.

6. Tax planning Tax planning is the process of organizing one's finances in a way that minimizes tax liability. Tax planning is an essential aspect of personal finance as it can help individuals to save money and maximize their income. In this section, we will discuss the different types of taxes, such as income tax, capital gains tax, and estate tax, and strategies for tax planning.

Overall, personal finance is an essential aspect of an individual's life, and it requires careful planning and management. By following the principles of personal finance and making informed financial decisions, individuals can achieve their financial goals and build a stable financial future.

Financial ratios

Introduction: Financial ratios are tools that are used to analyze and compare the financial statements of a company. They provide a systematic way to assess a company's performance, financial health, and efficiency. In this chapter, we will discuss the different types of financial ratios and their significance in analyzing a company's financial statements.

Types of Financial Ratios: Financial ratios are broadly classified into four categories: liquidity ratios, solvency ratios, profitability ratios, and efficiency ratios.

1. Liquidity Ratios: Liquidity ratios are used to assess a company's ability to meet its short-term obligations. These ratios measure the company's ability to convert its current assets into cash to meet its current liabilities. The most commonly used liquidity ratios are current ratio and quick ratio.

The current ratio is calculated by dividing current assets by current liabilities. A current ratio of 2 or higher indicates that the company has sufficient current assets to meet its current liabilities. A current ratio of less than 1 indicates that the company may have difficulty meeting its short-term obligations.

The quick ratio is calculated by dividing quick assets (current assets minus inventory) by current liabilities. The quick ratio is a more conservative measure of liquidity than the current ratio since it excludes inventory, which may take longer to convert into cash.

2. Solvency Ratios: Solvency ratios are used to assess a company's ability to meet its long-term obligations. These ratios measure the company's ability to repay its debt and interest on time. The most commonly used solvency ratios are debt-to-equity ratio and interest coverage ratio.

The debt-to-equity ratio is calculated by dividing total debt by total equity. A high debt-to-equity ratio indicates that the company is heavily reliant on debt to finance its operations, which can increase the company's financial risk.

The interest coverage ratio is calculated by dividing earnings before interest and taxes (EBIT) by interest expense. A high interest coverage ratio indicates that the company has sufficient earnings to cover its interest expense, which means it is less likely to default on its debt.

3. Profitability Ratios: Profitability ratios are used to assess a company's ability to generate profits from its operations. These ratios measure the company's profitability in relation to its sales, assets, and equity. The most commonly used profitability ratios are gross profit margin, net profit margin, return on assets (ROA), and return on equity (ROE).

The gross profit margin is calculated by dividing gross profit by sales. A high gross profit margin indicates that the company is able to generate a high level of profit from its sales.

The net profit margin is calculated by dividing net profit by sales. A high net profit margin indicates that the company is able to generate a high level of profit after deducting all expenses.

ROA is calculated by dividing net income by total assets. ROA measures the company's ability to generate profits from its assets.

ROE is calculated by dividing net income by total equity. ROE measures the company's ability to generate profits for its shareholders.

4. Efficiency Ratios: Efficiency ratios are used to assess a company's efficiency in managing its assets and liabilities. These ratios measure the company's ability to convert its assets into sales and its liabilities into cash. The most commonly used efficiency ratios are inventory turnover ratio, accounts receivable turnover ratio, and accounts payable turnover ratio.

The inventory turnover ratio is calculated by dividing the cost of goods sold by average inventory. The inventory turnover ratio measures the number of times the company's inventory is sold and replaced during a given period.

The accounts receivable turnover ratio is calculated by dividing sales by average accounts receivable. The accounts receivable turnover ratio measures the number of times the company's accounts receivable are collected during a given period.

*****

Another important financial ratio is the inventory turnover ratio, which measures how quickly a company sells its inventory. This ratio is calculated by dividing the cost of goods sold by the average inventory during a specific period. A high inventory turnover ratio is generally desirable, as it indicates that a company is selling its products quickly and efficiently.

The debt-to-equity ratio is another widely used financial ratio, which measures a company's debt relative to its equity. This ratio is calculated by dividing the company's total debt by its shareholder's equity. A high debt-to-equity ratio may indicate that a company is heavily leveraged, which can be risky if the company experiences financial difficulties.

The price-to-earnings (P/E) ratio is a widely used valuation ratio that compares a company's stock price to its earnings per share (EPS). This ratio is calculated by dividing the current stock price by the EPS. The P/E ratio is used by investors to evaluate the relative value of a company's stock and is an important tool for making investment decisions.

In addition to these ratios, there are several other financial ratios that can be used to evaluate a company's financial health and performance, including the current ratio, quick ratio, and return on equity (ROE) ratio. Understanding these ratios and how they are calculated can provide valuable insights into a company's financial position and help investors make informed decisions about whether to invest in a company.

Overall, financial ratios are an important tool for evaluating a company's financial health and performance. They provide a snapshot of a company's financial position and can help investors make informed decisions about whether to invest in a company. However, it is important to use financial ratios in conjunction with other forms of analysis, such as fundamental analysis and technical analysis, to gain a more comprehensive understanding of a company's financial health and potential for growth.

Time value of money

The time value of money is a crucial concept in finance, which states that the value of money today is not the same as the value of the same amount of money in the future. In other words, the value of money changes over time due to factors such as inflation, interest rates, and the opportunity cost of not investing that money elsewhere. Understanding the time value of money is essential for making informed financial decisions in areas such as investing, borrowing, and budgeting.

The time value of money is based on two main principles: the principle of compounding and the principle of discounting. The principle of compounding refers to the fact that money invested today will grow over time due to interest, and the interest earned will in turn earn more interest. The principle of discounting, on the other hand, is the inverse of compounding, and refers to the fact that the value of future money is less than the value of money today.

The time value of money can be illustrated using various financial tools, such as present value and future value calculations, annuities, and the calculation of interest rates. One of the most important tools for calculating the time value of money is the present value formula. The present value formula allows us to calculate the current value of a future sum of money based on a discount rate, which represents the rate of return that could be earned on an alternative investment of equivalent risk.

Another important tool for understanding the time value of money is annuities. An annuity is a series of payments made at regular intervals over a specified period of time. Annuities can be either ordinary annuities, where payments are made at the end of each period, or annuities due, where payments are made at the beginning of each period. The present value of an annuity can be calculated using the present value formula, and the future value of an annuity can be calculated using the future value formula.

Interest rates are also a key component of the time value of money. Interest rates represent the cost of borrowing money or the return on an investment. The time value of money tells us that money invested today will grow at a compounded rate over time, and therefore has a greater value in the future. Higher interest rates mean that money invested today will grow at a faster rate, while lower interest rates mean that the rate of growth will be slower.

In addition to investing, borrowing is another area where the time value of money is important. When borrowing money, interest is charged on the amount borrowed, and the borrower is required to pay back the principal amount plus interest over time. The interest rate charged by the lender represents the time value of money, as it reflects the cost of borrowing money over time.

Budgeting is another area where the time value of money is relevant. Budgeting involves planning how to allocate money over a period of time, taking into account the time value of money. This means considering the impact of inflation and interest rates on the purchasing power of money over time. By considering the time value of money, individuals and businesses can make better financial decisions, such as saving more for retirement or investing in assets that will appreciate in value over time.

In conclusion, the time value of money is a fundamental concept in finance that underlies many financial decisions. It is important to understand how the value of money changes over time due to factors such as inflation and interest rates, and how this affects financial decisions such as investing, borrowing, and budgeting. By taking into account the time value of money, individuals and businesses can make more informed financial decisions and improve their financial well-being.

Chapter 4: International Trade

Principles of international trade

International trade has been a crucial driver of global economic growth, contributing to an increase in living standards and the development of new markets. The principles of international trade are essential to understanding the dynamics of global commerce, including the benefits and challenges of engaging in international trade. This chapter will provide an overview of the fundamental principles of international trade, including the concept of comparative advantage, the gains from trade, and the different trade theories.

Concept of Comparative Advantage:

The concept of comparative advantage is a fundamental principle of international trade that explains why nations trade with one another. It is the ability of a country to produce a good or service at a lower opportunity cost than another country. Opportunity cost is the value of the next best alternative forgone in the production of a good or service. The theory of comparative advantage suggests that countries should specialize in producing the goods or services in which they have a comparative advantage and trade with other countries for goods or services in which they have a comparative disadvantage.

Gains from Trade:

The gains from trade refer to the net benefits that accrue to countries that engage in international trade. The gains from trade are based on the principle of comparative advantage, as countries can specialize in producing the goods or services in which they have a comparative advantage and trade with other countries for goods or services in which they have a comparative disadvantage. The gains from trade arise from the increased efficiency and productivity that result from specialization and the access to a greater variety of goods and services.

Trade Theories:

The different trade theories explain the reasons why countries engage in international trade and how international trade affects the economies of participating countries. The most important trade theories include the mercantilist theory, the classical theory, the Heckscher-Ohlin theory, and the new trade theory. The mercantilist theory emphasizes the importance of accumulating gold and silver reserves through exports and discouraging imports. The classical theory argues that free trade is beneficial for all countries, as it allows for the specialization of resources and the production of goods and services at a lower cost. The Heckscher-Ohlin theory suggests that countries specialize in producing goods that require factors of production that are abundant in their country, while importing goods that require factors of production that are scarce in their country. The new trade theory emphasizes the role of economies of scale and product differentiation in determining the pattern of international trade.

Trade Policies:

International trade is influenced by a range of policies, including trade barriers, subsidies, and exchange rate policies. Trade barriers, such as tariffs and quotas, are intended to protect domestic industries from foreign competition. Subsidies, on the other hand, are payments made by governments to domestic industries to promote exports or to provide a competitive advantage over foreign producers. Exchange rate policies, such as currency manipulation, can affect the competitiveness of a country's exports in international markets.

Conclusion:

The principles of international trade are crucial to understanding the dynamics of global commerce and the benefits and challenges of engaging in international trade. The concept of comparative advantage explains why countries trade with one another, and the gains from trade are based on the increased efficiency and productivity that result from specialization and access to a greater variety of goods and services. The different trade theories explain the reasons why countries engage in international trade and how it affects the economies of participating countries. Trade policies, such as trade barriers, subsidies, and exchange rate policies, can affect the competitiveness of a country's exports in international markets.

Tariffs and quotas

Tariffs and quotas are two of the most commonly used instruments of trade policy. They are used by governments to regulate international trade and protect domestic industries. While tariffs and quotas both aim to restrict the flow of imports, they work in different ways and have different effects on the economy. In this section, we will discuss the differences between tariffs and quotas, their economic effects, and the reasons why governments use them.

Tariffs A tariff is a tax imposed on imported goods. It increases the price of the imported goods, making them more expensive than domestic goods. This, in turn, makes domestic goods more competitive in the market. Tariffs can be specific, based on the quantity of the imported goods, or ad valorem, based on the value of the imported goods.

One of the primary reasons why governments use tariffs is to protect domestic industries from foreign competition. For example, if a country's steel industry is struggling to compete with cheaper imports from abroad, the government may impose a tariff on imported steel to make it more expensive and give the domestic industry a chance to compete. Tariffs can also be used to raise revenue for the government.

However, tariffs also have negative economic effects. First, they increase the price of imported goods, which can lead to inflation and reduce consumer purchasing power. Second, they can lead to retaliatory measures by trading partners, who may impose their own tariffs in response. This can lead to a trade war, which can hurt both countries involved. Finally, tariffs can lead to a misallocation of resources, as domestic industries that are protected by tariffs may become complacent and fail to innovate and become more efficient.

Quotas A quota is a limit on the quantity of a specific good that can be imported into a country. Unlike tariffs, quotas do not impose a tax on imports. Instead, they restrict the amount of imported goods that can enter the domestic market. Quotas can be voluntary, negotiated between two countries, or imposed unilaterally by a government.

Quotas are often used to protect domestic industries, just like tariffs. However, they have some advantages over tariffs. First, they do not increase the price of imports, so they are less likely to cause inflation and reduce consumer purchasing power. Second, they are less likely to lead to retaliatory measures by trading partners, as they do not involve the imposition of taxes on imports. Finally, they can be more effective at protecting domestic industries, as they restrict the actual quantity of imports, rather than just increasing their price.

However, quotas also have some disadvantages. First, they can lead to rent-seeking behavior, as domestic producers may try to obtain the limited import licenses and sell them at a higher price. This can lead to corruption and inefficiency. Second, quotas can lead to higher prices for consumers, as domestic producers may increase their prices to match the limited supply. Finally, quotas can also lead to a misallocation of resources, as domestic industries may become complacent and fail to innovate and become more efficient.

Conclusion In conclusion, tariffs and quotas are two of the most commonly used instruments of trade policy. While both aim to restrict the flow of imports, they work in different ways and have different economic effects. Tariffs impose a tax on imports, making them more expensive and protecting domestic industries. Quotas restrict the actual quantity of imports, making them less likely to cause inflation and retaliatory measures. However, both tariffs and quotas have negative economic effects, such as reducing consumer purchasing power, causing inflation, and leading to a misallocation of resources. Governments must carefully weigh the benefits and costs of using these trade policies before implementing them.

Exchange rates

Introduction: Exchange rates are a critical component of international trade and global finance. The exchange rate refers to the value of one currency in terms of another currency. For example, if the exchange rate between the U.S. dollar and the Euro is 1.20, it means that one U.S. dollar can be exchanged for 1.20 Euros. Exchange rates fluctuate over time due to various factors, including economic and political events, supply and demand, and central bank policies. In this article, we will explore exchange rates in more detail, including how they are determined, the types of exchange rates, and the factors that affect them.

Determinants of Exchange Rates: There are several factors that influence exchange rates. Some of the key determinants are as follows:

1. Interest rates: Interest rates play a significant role in determining exchange rates. When a country's interest rates are high, it attracts foreign investors who want to earn a higher return on their investments. As a result, there is an increased demand for that currency, causing its value to appreciate.

2. Economic indicators: Economic indicators such as gross domestic product (GDP), inflation, and unemployment rates can also impact exchange rates. A country with a strong economy is likely to have a stronger currency compared to a country with a weaker economy.

3. Political events: Political events, such as elections and geopolitical tensions, can also affect exchange rates. For example, if there is political uncertainty in a country, foreign investors may become hesitant to invest, causing the value of the currency to decline.

4. Supply and demand: Like any other market, exchange rates are also influenced by supply and demand. If there is a higher demand for a particular currency, its value will appreciate, and vice versa.

Types of Exchange Rates: There are several types of exchange rates that are used in the global economy. Some of the most common types are:

1. Spot exchange rate: The spot exchange rate refers to the current exchange rate at which two currencies can be traded in the market.

2. Forward exchange rate: A forward exchange rate is an agreement between two parties to exchange currencies at a fixed rate at a future date.

3. Real exchange rate: The real exchange rate is an adjusted exchange rate that takes into account the inflation rates of both countries.

4. Nominal exchange rate: The nominal exchange rate is the exchange rate without any adjustments for inflation.

Factors Affecting Exchange Rates: There are several factors that affect exchange rates. Some of the key factors are:

1. Central bank policies: Central bank policies, such as interest rates and money supply, can have a significant impact on exchange rates. For example, if a central bank increases interest rates, it can attract foreign investment, causing the value of the currency to appreciate.

2. Inflation rates: Inflation rates can also impact exchange rates. If a country has a higher inflation rate compared to other countries, its currency will likely depreciate.

3. Political stability: Political stability is an essential factor that affects exchange rates. If there is political uncertainty in a country, foreign investors may become hesitant to invest, causing the value of the currency to decline.

4. Trade balance: The trade balance of a country, which refers to the difference between exports and imports, can also affect exchange rates. A country with a trade surplus (i.e., exports more than it imports) will likely have a stronger currency compared to a country with a trade deficit.

Conclusion: Exchange rates are a critical component of the global economy and international trade. The value of currencies determines the cost of goods and services traded between countries. Understanding exchange rates and their determinants is essential for businesses and individuals involved in international trade and finance. The exchange rate is affected by various factors, including interest rates, economic indicators, political events, and supply and demand. The exchange rate system used by a country can also impact its economy and international trade relationships. A fixed exchange rate system provides stability and predictability but can lead to currency manipulation, while a floating exchange rate system allows for more flexibility but can lead to volatility. As global markets become increasingly interconnected, exchange rates continue to play a significant role in shaping the economic landscape. Businesses and individuals must be aware of exchange rate fluctuations and their potential impacts on trade and investments. Additionally, governments and central banks play a critical role in managing exchange rates and must carefully balance their objectives to maintain economic stability and promote international trade.

Balance of payments

Introduction: International trade involves the exchange of goods and services across borders. The balance of payments is a critical concept in international trade and finance that reflects the flow of money into and out of a country. It provides a comprehensive account of a country's economic transactions with the rest of the world, including imports and exports of goods and services, foreign investments, and other financial transactions. In this section, we will discuss the balance of payments, its components, and its significance in the global economy.

Components of the Balance of Payments: The balance of payments is divided into three main components: the current account, the capital account, and the financial account.

1. The Current Account: The current account measures the flow of goods and services between a country and the rest of the world. It includes the trade balance, which is the difference between the value of a country's exports and imports. If a country exports more than it imports, it has a trade surplus. If a country imports more than it exports, it has a trade deficit. The current account also includes the balance of services, which measures the value of services traded between countries, such as tourism, transportation, and financial services.

2. The Capital Account: The capital account measures the flow of capital between a country and the rest of the world. It includes direct investment, such as foreign companies

investing in a country's businesses, and portfolio investment, such as investments in stocks and bonds.

3. The Financial Account: The financial account measures the flow of financial assets and liabilities between a country and the rest of the world. It includes foreign direct investment, portfolio investment, and other financial transactions such as loans and currency swaps.

Significance of the Balance of Payments: The balance of payments is an essential tool for policymakers, investors, and businesses involved in international trade and finance. It provides valuable information on a country's economic performance and its relations with the rest of the world. A country with a surplus in the current account indicates that it is exporting more goods and services than it is importing, which can lead to an increase in foreign exchange reserves and a stronger currency. In contrast, a country with a deficit in the current account may indicate that it is importing more than it is exporting, which can lead to a weaker currency and a higher level of debt.

The balance of payments also helps policymakers make decisions about trade policies, such as tariffs and quotas. A country with a trade deficit may consider implementing policies to increase its exports and reduce its imports. Additionally, the balance of payments provides investors and businesses with insights into a country's economic outlook and can influence investment decisions.

Conclusion: The balance of payments is a crucial concept in international trade and finance that measures the flow of money into and out of a country. It is divided into three main components: the current account, the capital account, and the financial account. The balance of payments provides valuable information on a country's economic performance and its relations with the rest of the world. Policymakers, investors, and businesses can use this information to make informed decisions about trade policies and investment strategies.

Comparative advantage

Introduction: Comparative advantage is a fundamental concept in economics that explains the benefits of international trade. This concept suggests that countries should specialize in producing goods and services in which they have a lower opportunity cost and trade with other countries for goods and services that they cannot produce as efficiently. In this article, we will explore the concept of comparative advantage in detail, including its definition, theory, and applications.

Definition: Comparative advantage is the ability of a country to produce a particular good or service at a lower opportunity cost than another country. Opportunity cost refers to the value of the next best alternative that is forgone when a particular choice is made. It is the cost of the best alternative given up.

Theory: The theory of comparative advantage was first introduced by David Ricardo in his book "Principles of Political Economy and Taxation" in 1817. The theory suggests that if two countries specialize in producing the goods in which they have a comparative advantage, then they can trade with each other and both countries can benefit. The theory assumes that there are only two countries and two goods, and that there are no barriers to trade such as tariffs or quotas.

The theory can be explained using a simple example. Suppose there are two countries, A and B, and they can produce two goods, X and Y. The table below shows the production possibilities for each country.

Country	Good X	Good Y
A	10	5
B	5	10

Country A can produce 10 units of good X or 5 units of good Y. Country B can produce 5 units of good X or 10 units of good Y. According to the theory of comparative advantage, country A has a comparative advantage in producing good X, while country B has a comparative advantage in producing good Y.

To understand why, we need to calculate the opportunity cost for each country. The opportunity cost of producing one unit of good X in country A is 0.5 units of good Y (10/5), while the opportunity cost of producing one unit of good Y is 2 units of good X (5/10). The opportunity cost of producing one unit of good X in country B is 2 units of good Y (5/10), while the opportunity cost of producing one unit of good Y is 0.5 units of good X (10/5).

Based on the opportunity cost calculations, we can see that country A has a lower opportunity cost for producing good X than country B, while country B has a lower opportunity cost for producing good Y than country A. Therefore, country A should specialize in producing good X, while country B should specialize in producing good Y.

If each country specializes in producing the good in which it has a comparative advantage, then they can trade with each other. For example, country A can produce 20 units of good X and trade 10 units with country B for 10 units of good Y. Similarly, country B can produce 20 units of good Y and trade 10 units with country A for 10 units of good X. Both countries can now consume more of both goods than they could before trade.

Applications: The theory of comparative advantage has important applications in international trade. It suggests that countries can benefit from trade by specializing in producing the goods in which they have a comparative advantage and trading with other countries for goods that they cannot produce as efficiently.

The theory also suggests that free trade is beneficial for all countries involved. If countries impose trade barriers such as tariffs or quotas, then they are reducing the benefits of comparative advantage and restricting trade. Free trade allows countries to take advantage of their comparative advantages, which can lead to lower prices, increased output, and higher standards of living for all countries involved.

While comparative advantage is a valuable concept in theory, it is important to note that it is not without its limitations and criticisms. One criticism is that it assumes that resources are fully mobile within a country, but not between countries, which may not always be the case. It also assumes that there are no externalities, such as pollution or labor abuses, associated with the production of goods, which may not always be true in reality.

Despite these limitations, comparative advantage remains a fundamental principle in international trade and is often used as a justification for free trade policies. In practice, countries may use a variety of strategies to protect their domestic industries, including subsidies, tariffs, and quotas. However, the benefits of free trade, particularly the potential for increased efficiency and higher standards of living, suggest that efforts to promote comparative advantage and reduce trade barriers may be worth pursuing.

In conclusion, the concept of comparative advantage provides a useful framework for understanding the benefits of international trade and the potential for countries to specialize in the production of certain goods and services. While the theory has its limitations and criticisms, it remains an important principle in international economics and trade policy. By embracing free trade and allowing countries to take advantage of their comparative advantages, it is possible to achieve greater efficiency, lower prices, and higher standards of living for all involved.

WTO and global trade

Introduction: The World Trade Organization (WTO) is an international organization that promotes free trade and economic development. It provides a framework for negotiating and enforcing trade agreements, and it serves as a forum for resolving trade disputes among its member countries. In this section, we will discuss the role of the WTO in global trade, its history, structure, and functions, as well as its challenges and criticisms.

History: The WTO was established on January 1, 1995, as the successor to the General Agreement on Tariffs and Trade (GATT), which had been in existence since 1948. The GATT had played a critical role in promoting free trade and reducing tariffs among its member countries, but it was limited in its scope and lacked enforcement mechanisms. The WTO was designed to address these shortcomings and provide a more comprehensive and effective framework for international trade.

Structure: The WTO has a unique structure that includes a Ministerial Conference, a General Council, and several subsidiary bodies. The Ministerial Conference is the highest decision-making body and meets every two years to set the WTO's agenda and make policy decisions. The General Council is the WTO's main governing body and meets regularly to oversee the organization's activities. The subsidiary bodies, including committees on agriculture, services, and intellectual property, are responsible for negotiating and implementing specific trade agreements.

Functions: The WTO has several functions, including negotiating and implementing trade agreements, providing a forum for resolving trade disputes, and monitoring national trade policies. The WTO's most significant achievement is the creation of the multilateral trading system, which includes a set of rules and principles governing international trade. These rules promote free trade, reduce trade barriers, and provide a level playing field for all countries.

Dispute Settlement: One of the WTO's most critical functions is its dispute settlement system. The WTO's dispute settlement mechanism allows member countries to resolve trade disputes in a timely and efficient manner. The process begins with consultations between the parties involved and can escalate to a panel of experts and, ultimately, to the Appellate Body. The dispute settlement system has been successful in resolving many trade disputes and has helped prevent the escalation of conflicts between countries.

Challenges and Criticisms: The WTO faces several challenges and criticisms. Some critics argue that the WTO's rules and principles disproportionately favor developed countries and that the organization does not do enough to promote the interests of developing countries. Others argue that the WTO's focus on free trade and deregulation has contributed to income inequality, environmental degradation, and labor exploitation. There are also concerns about the WTO's effectiveness in addressing emerging trade issues, such as digital trade and intellectual property rights.

Conclusion: The WTO plays a vital role in promoting free trade and economic development, and its dispute settlement system has been successful in resolving many trade disputes. However, the organization faces several challenges and criticisms, and there are ongoing debates about the balance between free trade and other social and environmental goals. Despite these challenges, the WTO remains a critical institution for global trade, and its continued evolution and adaptation will be essential for addressing emerging trade issues and promoting sustainable economic growth.

Chapter 5: Public Policy
Role of government in the economy

Introduction: The role of government in the economy is a central issue in public policy. Governments have a critical role in shaping economic growth and development, regulating markets, providing public goods and services, and promoting social welfare. The extent and nature of government intervention in the economy have varied across countries and historical periods. In this chapter, we will discuss the role of government in the economy, the different forms of government intervention, and the advantages and disadvantages of government intervention in the economy.

Market Failures: One of the primary justifications for government intervention in the economy is the presence of market failures. Market failures occur when the market fails to allocate resources efficiently, resulting in inefficiencies, inequities, and negative externalities. Examples of market failures include monopolies, externalities, public goods, and information asymmetry. In these cases, government intervention can correct market failures and improve economic outcomes. For example, governments can regulate monopolies, provide public goods, and impose taxes on negative externalities.

Forms of Government Intervention: Governments can intervene in the economy in various ways, including fiscal policy, monetary policy, regulation, and public provision of goods and services. Fiscal policy involves the use of government spending and taxation to influence aggregate demand and stabilize the economy. Monetary policy involves the use of interest rates and the money supply to influence economic growth and inflation. Regulation involves the imposition of rules and standards on businesses to protect consumers, workers, and the environment. The public provision of goods and services involves the government's direct provision of essential goods and services, such as education, healthcare, and infrastructure.

Advantages of Government Intervention: Government intervention in the economy can have several advantages. For example, government intervention can correct market failures and promote efficiency and equity. It can also provide essential public goods and services that the market may not provide, such as healthcare, education, and infrastructure. Government intervention can also promote economic growth and development by investing in human capital, supporting innovation and entrepreneurship, and providing stable macroeconomic conditions.

Disadvantages of Government Intervention: Government intervention in the economy can also have disadvantages. One of the primary disadvantages is the risk of government failure, which occurs when government intervention leads to inefficiencies, ineffectiveness, and unintended consequences. Government intervention can also lead to distortions in the market and create moral hazards, where individuals and businesses may take excessive risks or engage in harmful behavior due to the presence of government support or insurance. Government intervention can also be costly and lead to higher taxes, lower incentives, and reduced economic freedom.

Conclusion: The role of government in the economy is complex and multifaceted. Governments have a critical role in correcting market failures, promoting efficiency and equity, and providing essential public goods and services. However, government intervention can also lead to unintended consequences, distortions, and inefficiencies. The optimal level and form of government intervention in the economy depend on various factors, including the nature of market failures, political and institutional factors, and the goals and values of society. Therefore, public policy must balance the benefits and costs of government intervention and strive to achieve the most efficient and equitable outcomes for society.

Monetary policy

Monetary policy is a tool used by the government to regulate the supply and demand of money in an economy. It involves the management of the money supply, interest rates, and credit conditions to achieve specific economic goals. The primary objectives of monetary policy are to maintain price stability, promote economic growth, and stabilize financial markets. In this article, we will discuss the basics of monetary policy, its objectives, and the different types of monetary policy tools used by governments.

Objectives of Monetary Policy The primary objective of monetary policy is to maintain price stability. Price stability refers to a situation where the general level of prices of goods and services in the economy remains stable over time. It means that there is no significant inflation or deflation in the economy. The central bank aims to achieve this by controlling the money supply, interest rates, and credit conditions.

The second objective of monetary policy is to promote economic growth. The central bank aims to achieve this by controlling interest rates and credit conditions. Lower interest rates and easier credit conditions stimulate borrowing and spending, which can lead to increased economic activity.

The third objective of monetary policy is to stabilize financial markets. This is achieved by ensuring that financial institutions are stable and that the financial system is functioning properly. The central bank can use a variety of tools to achieve this, including providing liquidity to the financial system and regulating financial institutions.

Types of Monetary Policy Tools There are two main types of monetary policy tools: conventional and unconventional.

Conventional Monetary Policy Tools Conventional monetary policy tools include open market operations, discount rate policy, and reserve requirements.

Open market operations involve the buying and selling of government securities by the central bank in the open market. When the central bank buys government securities, it injects money into the economy, increasing the money supply. When it sells government securities, it removes money from the economy, decreasing the money supply.

Discount rate policy refers to the interest rate that the central bank charges commercial banks for borrowing money. When the central bank lowers the discount rate, it makes it cheaper for commercial banks to borrow money, which can stimulate borrowing and spending in the economy.

Reserve requirements refer to the amount of money that banks are required to hold in reserve against their deposits. When the central bank increases reserve requirements, it reduces the amount of money that banks can lend, which can decrease borrowing and spending in the economy.

Unconventional Monetary Policy Tools Unconventional monetary policy tools include quantitative easing (QE) and forward guidance.

Quantitative easing refers to the purchase of long-term government bonds or other securities by the central bank to increase the money supply and lower long-term interest rates. This is done when conventional monetary policy tools have reached their limits.

Forward guidance involves the central bank providing guidance to financial markets about the future path of monetary policy. This can be used to influence market expectations and help steer the economy towards the desired outcome.

Conclusion Monetary policy is a powerful tool used by governments to manage the economy. By regulating the supply and demand of money, interest rates, and credit conditions, governments can achieve specific economic goals. The primary objectives of monetary policy are to maintain price stability, promote economic growth, and stabilize financial markets. Conventional and unconventional monetary policy tools can be used to achieve these objectives, depending on the economic situation.

Regulatory policy

Introduction: Regulatory policy refers to the laws, rules, and guidelines that governments create to regulate various aspects of society, including businesses, industries, and individuals. Regulatory policies can have a significant impact on the economy by promoting competition, protecting consumers, and ensuring public safety. In this article, we will discuss the importance of regulatory policy, the types of regulations that exist, and the role of government in regulating various sectors of the economy.

Importance of Regulatory Policy: Regulatory policy plays a crucial role in ensuring that businesses and individuals operate in a fair and safe environment. Regulations help to promote competition by preventing monopolies and reducing barriers to entry for new businesses. They also protect consumers by setting standards for product safety and quality, and ensuring that businesses are transparent and accountable.

Furthermore, regulatory policies help to maintain public trust in various industries by ensuring that businesses and individuals act in a socially responsible manner. For example, regulations on environmental protection ensure that businesses do not harm the environment through their activities. Regulatory policies also help to promote social welfare by protecting vulnerable groups and ensuring that all individuals have access to essential goods and services.

Types of Regulations: Regulations can be classified into various types, including economic, social, and environmental regulations. Economic regulations are laws that regulate market competition and pricing. These regulations are aimed at preventing monopolies and reducing barriers to entry for new businesses. Examples of economic regulations include antitrust laws, minimum wage laws, and price controls.

Social regulations are laws that protect consumers and promote public safety. These regulations set standards for product safety and quality, and ensure that businesses are transparent and accountable. Examples of social regulations include regulations on food safety, workplace safety, and consumer protection.

Environmental regulations are laws that protect the environment from the harmful effects of human activities. These regulations are aimed at reducing pollution, conserving natural resources, and promoting sustainable development. Examples of environmental regulations include regulations on air and water pollution, hazardous waste disposal, and conservation of biodiversity.

Role of Government: The role of government in regulating various sectors of the economy is crucial. The government creates and enforces regulations to ensure that businesses and individuals operate in a fair and safe environment. Governments also play a critical role in enforcing regulations and penalizing individuals and businesses that violate them.

Furthermore, the government has the responsibility to balance the benefits of regulations against their costs. Regulations can impose costs on businesses and individuals, such as compliance costs, which can reduce their competitiveness. The government must weigh these costs against the benefits of regulations, such as increased competition, improved public safety, and environmental protection.

The government also has a role in ensuring that regulations are effective and efficient. Regulatory agencies are responsible for monitoring compliance with regulations and enforcing penalties when necessary. These agencies also play a role in evaluating the effectiveness of regulations and making changes to them as needed.

Conclusion: Regulatory policy is an essential aspect of government policy that plays a crucial role in promoting competition, protecting consumers, and ensuring public safety. Regulations can have a significant impact on the economy, and it is essential that they are created and enforced in a manner that balances their benefits against their costs. Governments must play an active role in regulating various sectors of the economy to ensure that businesses and individuals operate in a fair and safe environment.

Antitrust policy

Antitrust policy refers to the measures taken by the government to promote competition in the market and prevent monopolies or anti-competitive behavior by companies. The goal of antitrust policy is to protect consumer welfare by ensuring that firms do not engage in practices that harm competition, such as price fixing, bid rigging, market allocation, or tying arrangements. This article discusses the principles of antitrust policy, its objectives, and the legal framework for antitrust enforcement.

Objectives of Antitrust Policy

The primary objective of antitrust policy is to promote competition in the market. Competition is essential for efficient allocation of resources, lower prices, and higher output. When companies compete, they are forced to innovate, improve their products, and lower their costs. This leads to better products and services at lower prices for consumers.

Antitrust policy also aims to prevent monopolies or anti-competitive behavior by firms. A monopoly is a situation where a single company dominates the market, and there are no close substitutes for its product. In such cases, the monopolist can charge higher prices and reduce output, which harms consumers. Antitrust policy aims to prevent the abuse of market power by firms and promote competition.

Principles of Antitrust Policy

The principles of antitrust policy are based on economic theory and legal precedent. The following are the main principles of antitrust policy:

1. Market power: Antitrust policy focuses on firms that have significant market power. Market power is the ability of a firm to control prices or output in a market. Firms with market power can harm consumers by charging higher prices or reducing output.

2. Harm to competition: Antitrust policy is concerned with practices that harm competition. Examples of such practices include price fixing, bid rigging, market allocation, and tying arrangements. These practices can reduce competition and lead to higher prices and reduced output.

3. Consumer welfare: Antitrust policy aims to protect consumer welfare by promoting competition. When firms compete, consumers benefit from lower prices, better products, and greater choice. Antitrust policy aims to prevent practices that harm consumers, such as price fixing or monopolization.

4. Legal framework: Antitrust policy is based on legal frameworks that prohibit anti-competitive practices. In the United States, antitrust policy is governed by the Sherman Antitrust Act, the Clayton Antitrust Act, and the Federal Trade Commission Act. These laws prohibit practices that harm competition and provide for civil and criminal penalties for violations.

Antitrust Enforcement

Antitrust enforcement is the process of investigating and prosecuting firms that engage in anti-competitive practices. Antitrust enforcement is carried out by government agencies such as the Federal Trade Commission (FTC) or the Department of Justice (DOJ) in the United States. The following are the main tools of antitrust enforcement:

1. Investigations: Antitrust agencies conduct investigations to determine whether firms are engaging in anti-competitive practices. Investigations can involve reviewing documents, interviewing witnesses, and analyzing market data.

2. Remedies: Antitrust agencies can impose remedies on firms that engage in anti-competitive practices. Remedies can include divestitures, injunctions, or fines.

3. Litigation: Antitrust agencies can bring lawsuits against firms that engage in anti-competitive practices. Lawsuits can lead to injunctions or fines.

Antitrust policy is a crucial tool for promoting competition in the market and protecting consumer welfare. By preventing anti-competitive practices, antitrust policy promotes innovation, lower prices, and better products and services for consumers.

Environmental policy

Environmental policy is a critical component of public policy, aimed at protecting the environment and promoting sustainable development. Environmental policy seeks to address environmental issues such as climate change, pollution, and conservation of natural resources. In recent years, environmental policy has gained significant importance due to the increased awareness of the impacts of human activities on the environment. This article will explore the key concepts and issues related to environmental policy, including the history of environmental policy, the main approaches to environmental policy, and the challenges faced in implementing environmental policy.

History of Environmental Policy:

The history of environmental policy can be traced back to the early 20th century when concerns about air and water pollution started to emerge. The United States was one of the first countries to develop environmental policies, with the establishment of the National Park Service in 1916 and the Clean Air Act in 1963. The first Earth Day was celebrated in 1970, which marked the beginning of the modern environmental movement.

In the following decades, many countries around the world developed their environmental policies, and international agreements such as the United Nations Framework Convention on Climate Change (UNFCCC) and the Paris Agreement were established to address global environmental issues. The UNFCCC was signed in 1992 and aimed to prevent dangerous human interference with the climate system, while the Paris Agreement, signed in 2015, aimed to keep the global temperature rise below 2°C.

Approaches to Environmental Policy:

There are several approaches to environmental policy, including command-and-control, market-based, and collaborative approaches.

Command-and-control approaches involve setting specific environmental standards and regulations that must be met by firms or individuals. This approach is often criticized for being inflexible and costly, as it does not allow for innovation or flexibility in meeting environmental targets.

Market-based approaches aim to create economic incentives for firms or individuals to reduce their environmental impact. These incentives can include taxes, subsidies, and emissions trading systems. Market-based approaches are generally seen as more flexible and cost-effective than command-and-control approaches.

Collaborative approaches involve working with stakeholders such as industry groups, non-governmental organizations, and community groups to develop and implement environmental policies. This approach is often seen as a way to build consensus and achieve more sustainable outcomes.

Challenges in Implementing Environmental Policy:

Implementing effective environmental policy can be challenging due to several factors. One major challenge is the complexity of environmental issues, which can involve multiple stakeholders and require interdisciplinary approaches. Additionally, there may be political opposition to environmental policies, particularly from industries that may be impacted by regulations.

Another challenge is ensuring compliance with environmental regulations. Enforcement mechanisms must be in place to ensure that firms and individuals comply with environmental standards and regulations.

Finally, the costs of implementing environmental policies can be a significant challenge. Some stakeholders may resist policies that increase their costs, and there may be concerns about the economic impacts of environmental policies.

Conclusion:

Environmental policy is an essential component of public policy, aimed at protecting the environment and promoting sustainable development. The history of environmental policy can be traced back to the early 20th century, and in recent decades, many countries around the world have developed their environmental policies. There are several approaches to environmental policy, including command-and-control, market-based, and collaborative approaches, each with its advantages and disadvantages. Implementing effective environmental policy can be challenging, but with interdisciplinary approaches, enforcement mechanisms, and careful consideration of costs and benefits, it is possible to develop policies that promote environmental sustainability.

Social welfare policy

Introduction: Social welfare policy is a critical aspect of public policy, designed to promote the well-being of individuals and families in need. The policy aims to provide social and economic support to people who are unable to support themselves, including the elderly, the disabled, and low-income families. The social welfare policy has evolved over time, reflecting changes in social, economic, and political conditions. This article provides an overview of social welfare policy, including its history, types, and challenges.

History of Social Welfare Policy: The origins of social welfare policy can be traced back to ancient civilizations, where rulers provided food, shelter, and clothing to their subjects in times of need. In the United States, social welfare policy emerged in the early 20th century, during the progressive era. Social welfare programs were designed to address the social and economic problems caused by industrialization, including poverty, unemployment, and social unrest. The first social welfare program in the United States was the Social Security Act of 1935, which provided financial assistance to elderly citizens and the disabled.

Types of Social Welfare Policy: Social welfare policy encompasses a range of programs designed to support people in need. Some of the most common types of social welfare policy include:

1. Healthcare Policy: Healthcare policy aims to provide access to quality healthcare to all citizens, regardless of their income level. The Affordable Care Act of 2010 is an example of a healthcare policy in the United States.

2. Housing Policy: Housing policy aims to provide safe, affordable housing to low-income families. Programs such as Section 8 housing vouchers and public housing are examples of housing policies in the United States.

3. Income Support Policy: Income support policy provides financial assistance to individuals and families in need. Programs such as Temporary Assistance for Needy Families (TANF) and Supplemental Nutrition Assistance Program (SNAP) are examples of income support policies in the United States.

4. Child Welfare Policy: Child welfare policy aims to protect children from abuse and neglect and provide them with safe, stable homes. Programs such as foster care and adoption services are examples of child welfare policies in the United States.

Challenges of Social Welfare Policy: Social welfare policy faces a range of challenges, including:

1. Funding: Social welfare programs require significant funding to operate, which can be a challenge in times of economic downturn or political opposition.

2. Eligibility Requirements: Eligibility requirements for social welfare programs can be complex and difficult to

navigate, making it difficult for people in need to access the support they require.

3. Stigma: There can be a stigma associated with receiving social welfare support, which can deter some individuals and families from seeking the help they need.

4. Political Opposition: Social welfare policies are often subject to political opposition, particularly in times of economic uncertainty or political polarization.

Conclusion: Social welfare policy plays a critical role in promoting the well-being of individuals and families in need. The policy has evolved over time, reflecting changes in social, economic, and political conditions. Healthcare, housing, income support, and child welfare are among the most common types of social welfare policies. However, social welfare policy faces a range of challenges, including funding, eligibility requirements, stigma, and political opposition. Despite these challenges, social welfare policy remains a critical component of public policy, designed to support the most vulnerable members of society.

Chapter 6: Accounting

Principles of accounting

Principles of accounting refer to the fundamental concepts, rules, and procedures that guide the preparation, presentation, and interpretation of financial statements. These principles are crucial in providing accurate and reliable financial information that can be used by various stakeholders, including investors, creditors, regulators, and management.

The following are the primary principles of accounting:

1. Accrual basis accounting: The accrual basis of accounting recognizes revenues and expenses when they are earned or incurred, regardless of when the cash is received or paid. This method provides a more accurate picture of a company's financial performance since it reflects the economic activity of the business during a given period.

2. Going concern: The going concern principle assumes that a business will continue to operate indefinitely. This assumption is vital in financial reporting since it provides a basis for valuing assets, estimating liabilities, and assessing the company's ability to meet its financial obligations.

3. Consistency: Consistency requires that a company uses the same accounting methods and procedures from one period to the next. This principle helps ensure that financial statements are comparable over time, making it easier for investors and other stakeholders to assess a company's financial performance.

4. Materiality: Materiality requires that a company only report financial information that is significant enough to influence the decisions of users of the financial statements. This principle allows companies to avoid reporting trivial or immaterial information that could clutter financial statements and make it harder for users to understand the company's financial performance.

5. Conservatism: Conservatism requires that a company report all potential losses immediately but only report potential gains when they are realized. This principle helps companies avoid overstating their financial performance by only recognizing gains that are certain, while recognizing losses that are only potential.

6. Objectivity: Objectivity requires that financial information be based on objective evidence and free from bias or personal opinion. This principle helps ensure that financial statements are reliable and can be trusted by investors and other stakeholders.

7. Full disclosure: Full disclosure requires that a company provide all relevant financial information in its financial statements and footnotes. This principle helps ensure that investors and other stakeholders have access to all the information they need to make informed decisions about a company's financial performance and future prospects.

In conclusion, these principles of accounting provide a framework for preparing and presenting financial information that is accurate, reliable, and useful for various stakeholders. By following these principles, companies can provide transparency and accountability, which can enhance their reputation and attract investors and creditors.

Financial statements

Introduction: Financial statements are a set of reports that provide important financial information about a company. They are used by investors, creditors, and other stakeholders to assess a company's financial performance and make informed decisions. In this article, we will discuss the different types of financial statements and their significance in accounting.

Types of Financial Statements: There are four main types of financial statements: the balance sheet, income statement, cash flow statement, and statement of shareholders' equity. Each of these statements provides a different perspective on a company's financial performance and position.

1. Balance Sheet: The balance sheet is a snapshot of a company's financial position at a specific point in time. It lists the company's assets, liabilities, and shareholders' equity. Assets are the resources owned by the company, while liabilities are the company's debts or obligations. Shareholders' equity represents the amount of capital invested by shareholders.

The balance sheet is important because it shows how the company's resources are financed. If a company has more liabilities than assets, it may have trouble meeting its financial obligations. Conversely, if a company has more assets than liabilities, it may have excess cash or other resources that can be used for future investments.

2. Income Statement: The income statement, also known as the profit and loss statement, provides information

about a company's revenue, expenses, and net income over a specific period of time. Revenue is the money the company earns from its operations, while expenses are the costs associated with generating that revenue.

The income statement is important because it shows whether a company is profitable or not. If a company has a positive net income, it means that it earned more revenue than it spent on expenses. On the other hand, if a company has a negative net income, it means that it spent more on expenses than it earned in revenue.

3. Cash Flow Statement: The cash flow statement provides information about a company's cash inflows and outflows over a specific period of time. It shows how much cash the company generated from its operations, how much it invested in capital expenditures, and how much it paid out in dividends or other expenses.

The cash flow statement is important because it shows whether a company is generating cash from its operations. A company may have a positive net income, but if it is not generating cash, it may not be able to meet its financial obligations.

4. Statement of Shareholders' Equity: The statement of shareholders' equity provides information about changes in a company's shareholders' equity over a specific period of time. It shows how much capital was invested by shareholders, how

much was earned in profits, and how much was paid out in dividends.

The statement of shareholders' equity is important because it shows how much the company's shareholders' equity has changed over time. If a company is consistently paying out dividends or buying back shares, it may be an indication that the company is doing well and has excess cash to distribute to its shareholders.

Conclusion: Financial statements are essential tools for assessing a company's financial performance and position. They provide important information about a company's assets, liabilities, revenue, expenses, cash flows, and shareholders' equity. By analyzing these statements, investors, creditors, and other stakeholders can make informed decisions about a company's future prospects and financial stability.

Auditing

Introduction: Auditing is a crucial function in accounting, providing independent and objective assurance to stakeholders that financial statements are presented accurately and fairly. The primary objective of auditing is to provide reasonable assurance to stakeholders that the financial statements are free from material misstatement. In this article, we will explore the concept of auditing, its objectives, types of audit, and the auditing process.

Objectives of Auditing: The objectives of auditing are as follows:

1. To express an opinion on the fairness of the financial statements: The primary objective of auditing is to express an opinion on the financial statements' fairness and accuracy.

2. To detect material misstatement: The auditor's responsibility is to detect and report any material misstatement in the financial statements that could mislead the stakeholders.

3. To assess the adequacy of internal controls: Auditors are required to evaluate the company's internal controls and assess whether they are adequate to prevent and detect material misstatements.

4. To comply with legal and regulatory requirements: Auditors are required to comply with legal and regulatory requirements, such as the Sarbanes-Oxley Act, to ensure that the financial statements are prepared in accordance with generally accepted accounting principles.

Types of Audits: There are several types of audits, and each type serves a specific purpose. The most common types of audits are:

1. Financial Statement Audit: A financial statement audit is the most common type of audit, where auditors review and evaluate a company's financial statements to express an opinion on their fairness and accuracy.

2. Compliance Audit: Compliance audits ensure that a company complies with legal and regulatory requirements, such as tax laws, environmental regulations, and labor laws.

3. Operational Audit: Operational audits evaluate the efficiency and effectiveness of a company's operations and processes, such as manufacturing processes or supply chain management.

4. Forensic Audit: Forensic audits are conducted to detect and investigate fraud or other illegal activities.

Auditing Process: The auditing process involves several steps that must be followed to ensure the accuracy and completeness of the audit.

1. Planning: The first step in the auditing process is planning, where the auditor evaluates the risks associated with the audit and develops an audit plan.

2. Internal Control Evaluation: The auditor evaluates the company's internal controls to ensure that they are adequate to prevent and detect material misstatements.

3. Testing: The auditor tests the financial statements and supporting documents to detect any material misstatements.

4. Reporting: The auditor prepares a report detailing the audit findings, including any material misstatements detected.

Conclusion: In conclusion, auditing is a crucial function in accounting, providing independent and objective assurance to stakeholders that financial statements are presented accurately and fairly. Auditors are responsible for detecting material misstatements and assessing the adequacy of internal controls to prevent and detect such misstatements. The auditing process involves several steps, including planning, internal control evaluation, testing, and reporting. It is essential to conduct audits regularly to ensure the accuracy and integrity of financial statements and maintain the trust of stakeholders.

Managerial accounting

Managerial accounting is the process of analyzing and interpreting financial information for the purpose of making business decisions. The focus of managerial accounting is on providing information to internal users, such as managers and employees, rather than to external stakeholders, such as investors and creditors. This chapter will provide an overview of managerial accounting and the role it plays in helping businesses make informed decisions.

Overview of Managerial Accounting:

Managerial accounting is a broad term that encompasses various accounting practices, such as cost accounting, budgeting, and forecasting. The goal of managerial accounting is to provide information to internal users to help them make informed decisions. This information includes financial and non-financial data, such as sales trends, production costs, and employee productivity.

Managerial accounting involves the following processes:

1. Planning: This involves setting goals and objectives for the business and developing a strategy to achieve them. This process includes preparing budgets, forecasts, and projections.

2. Controlling: This involves monitoring the performance of the business and taking corrective action when necessary. This process includes analyzing financial and operational data, such as sales figures and production costs.

3. Decision-making: This involves using the information gathered during the planning and controlling processes to make informed business decisions. This process includes analyzing financial and non-financial data, such as market trends and consumer preferences.

Cost Accounting:

Cost accounting is the process of measuring, analyzing, and reporting the costs of production. Cost accounting provides information about the costs of raw materials, labor, and overhead, which can help businesses determine the cost of producing their products or services. This information can also be used to identify areas where costs can be reduced or eliminated.

Budgeting:

Budgeting is the process of creating a financial plan for the business. Budgets can be used to plan for future expenses, such as capital investments, marketing campaigns, and research and development projects. Budgets can also be used to track actual expenses and compare them to the budgeted amounts.

Forecasting:

Forecasting involves using past data and trends to predict future events. Businesses use forecasting to predict future sales, expenses, and profits. This information can be used to make informed decisions about the future direction of the business.

Performance Measurement:

Performance measurement involves evaluating the performance of the business against its goals and objectives. This process includes analyzing financial and non-financial data, such as sales figures, customer satisfaction, and employee productivity. Performance measurement can be used to identify areas where the business is performing well and areas where improvements can be made.

Conclusion:

Managerial accounting is an essential tool for businesses looking to make informed decisions. By providing information about costs, budgets, forecasts, and performance, managerial accounting helps businesses identify areas where they can improve their operations and make better use of their resources. With the help of managerial accounting, businesses can improve their efficiency, reduce costs, and increase profitability.

Cost accounting

Cost accounting is an important aspect of managerial accounting that involves the process of collecting, analyzing, and interpreting data related to the costs incurred by a business. The aim of cost accounting is to help businesses make informed decisions related to pricing, budgeting, and cost control. In this article, we will discuss the key concepts and methods used in cost accounting.

Cost Accounting Concepts:

1. Cost: Cost refers to the amount of resources, such as money, time, and effort, that are consumed in the production of a product or service.

2. Direct costs: Direct costs are expenses that are directly associated with the production of a specific product or service. Examples of direct costs include raw materials, labor, and shipping costs.

3. Indirect costs: Indirect costs are expenses that are not directly associated with the production of a specific product or service but are necessary for the operation of the business. Examples of indirect costs include rent, utilities, and office supplies.

4. Fixed costs: Fixed costs are expenses that remain constant regardless of the level of production. Examples of fixed costs include rent, insurance, and salaries.

5. Variable costs: Variable costs are expenses that change in proportion to the level of production. Examples of variable costs include raw materials, labor, and shipping costs.

Cost Accounting Methods:

1. Job order costing: Job order costing is a method of cost accounting that is used to determine the cost of a specific job or project. This method is commonly used in industries such as construction, manufacturing, and consulting.

2. Process costing: Process costing is a method of cost accounting that is used to determine the cost of a product or service that is produced in large quantities. This method is commonly used in industries such as food production and chemical manufacturing.

3. Activity-based costing: Activity-based costing is a method of cost accounting that is used to determine the cost of a product or service by identifying the activities that are required to produce it. This method is commonly used in industries such as healthcare and financial services.

Cost Accounting Techniques:

1. Marginal costing: Marginal costing is a technique that involves the separation of fixed and variable costs. This technique is useful for determining the contribution margin of a product or service, which is the difference between its selling price and variable costs.

2. Standard costing: Standard costing is a technique that involves the establishment of standard costs for materials,

labor, and overhead. This technique is useful for comparing actual costs to predetermined standards and identifying areas for improvement.

3. Cost-volume-profit analysis: Cost-volume-profit analysis is a technique that is used to determine the break-even point for a product or service. This technique is useful for determining the amount of revenue that is required to cover the fixed and variable costs of production.

Conclusion:

Cost accounting is an important tool for businesses to make informed decisions related to pricing, budgeting, and cost control. The key concepts, methods, and techniques discussed in this article provide businesses with the tools they need to analyze and understand their costs. By implementing effective cost accounting practices, businesses can improve their profitability and competitiveness in the marketplace.

Tax accounting is a specialized branch of accounting that deals with the preparation, analysis, and filing of tax returns. Tax accounting is essential for individuals and businesses to ensure that they are compliant with tax laws and regulations and to minimize their tax liabilities. In this article, we will discuss the key concepts of tax accounting, including the types of taxes, tax planning strategies, and tax compliance.

Types of Taxes: There are several types of taxes that individuals and businesses are required to pay. These include income tax, sales tax, property tax, payroll tax, and excise tax. The rules and regulations governing each type of tax can vary depending on the jurisdiction, and it is essential to understand the specific requirements for each tax.

Income tax is a tax levied on an individual's or business's income, including wages, salaries, interest, dividends, capital gains, and business profits. Income tax is one of the most significant sources of revenue for governments and is used to fund public services and programs.

Sales tax is a tax levied on the sale of goods and services. Sales tax is typically imposed at the state or local level and can vary depending on the jurisdiction. Businesses are responsible for collecting and remitting sales tax to the appropriate government agency.

Property tax is a tax levied on real estate and other property owned by individuals and businesses. Property tax rates can vary depending on the jurisdiction and the value of the property.

Payroll tax is a tax levied on wages and salaries paid by employers. Employers are responsible for withholding payroll taxes from employees' paychecks and remitting them to the appropriate government agency.

Excise tax is a tax levied on specific goods and services, such as gasoline, tobacco, and alcohol. Excise tax is typically included in the price of the product and is collected by the retailer.

Tax Planning: Tax planning involves the use of various strategies to minimize tax liabilities while complying with tax laws and regulations. Tax planning can include strategies such as:

1. Taking advantage of tax deductions and credits: Tax deductions and credits can reduce the amount of income subject to tax, reducing the overall tax liability.

2. Deferring income: Deferring income to future tax years can reduce the current tax liability.

3. Using tax-exempt investments: Investing in tax-exempt securities, such as municipal bonds, can provide tax-free income.

4. Structuring business transactions: Structuring business transactions in a tax-efficient manner can reduce the overall tax liability.

Tax Compliance: Tax compliance involves the preparation, analysis, and filing of tax returns to ensure that individuals and businesses are compliant with tax laws and regulations. Tax compliance can be complex and time-consuming, requiring a thorough understanding of tax laws and regulations.

To ensure compliance, individuals and businesses must keep accurate records of their income and expenses, report all income to the appropriate government agency, and file tax returns on time. Failure to comply with tax laws and regulations can result in penalties and fines.

In addition to complying with tax laws and regulations, individuals and businesses must also be aware of changes in tax laws and regulations that may affect their tax liabilities. Tax laws and regulations can change frequently, and it is essential to stay up-to-date with the latest changes.

Conclusion: Tax accounting is a critical component of accounting that involves the preparation, analysis, and filing of tax returns. Tax accounting is essential for individuals and businesses to ensure that they are compliant with tax laws and regulations and to minimize their tax liabilities. Understanding the types of taxes, tax planning strategies, and tax compliance requirements is essential for individuals and businesses to manage their tax obligations effectively.

Chapter 7: Business Ethics
Principles of business ethics

Business ethics refers to the set of moral and ethical principles that guide the behavior and actions of individuals and organizations in the business world. These principles are essential for maintaining the trust and confidence of stakeholders, including customers, employees, investors, and the wider community. In this article, we will explore the key principles of business ethics and their significance in the modern business environment.

1. Integrity Integrity is the fundamental principle of business ethics. It means doing what is right, even when it is difficult or unpopular. It is about being honest, transparent, and ethical in all business dealings. Integrity is essential for building trust and credibility with stakeholders, including customers, employees, and investors.

2. Responsibility Responsibility refers to the duty of businesses to act in the best interests of all stakeholders. This includes being accountable for the social, environmental, and economic impact of their actions. Responsibility also means taking steps to mitigate any harm caused by business operations and promoting positive outcomes for all stakeholders.

3. Fairness Fairness is the principle of treating all stakeholders equally and without discrimination. It means providing equal opportunities and benefits to all employees,

customers, and suppliers, regardless of their race, gender, or other personal characteristics. Fairness also includes avoiding any form of favoritism or bias in decision-making.

4. Respect Respect is the principle of treating all stakeholders with dignity and respect. It means valuing the opinions, rights, and interests of all individuals and groups and avoiding any form of harassment, discrimination, or exploitation. Respect also includes promoting diversity and inclusion in the workplace and the wider community.

5. Transparency Transparency is the principle of being open and honest in all business dealings. It means providing accurate and timely information to stakeholders about business operations, financial performance, and any potential risks or challenges. Transparency also includes promoting accountability and taking responsibility for any mistakes or errors.

6. Sustainability Sustainability is the principle of balancing economic growth with social and environmental responsibility. It means taking steps to minimize the negative impact of business operations on the environment and society, while also promoting long-term economic growth and profitability. Sustainability includes implementing environmentally friendly practices, supporting social initiatives, and promoting ethical business practices.

7. Compliance Compliance is the principle of following all laws, regulations, and ethical standards applicable to

business operations. It means maintaining high ethical standards and avoiding any form of illegal or unethical behavior. Compliance also includes promoting ethical behavior among employees and taking steps to prevent and detect any form of misconduct or corruption.

In conclusion, the principles of business ethics provide a framework for ethical behavior and decision-making in the business world. By following these principles, businesses can build trust and credibility with stakeholders, promote social and environmental responsibility, and achieve long-term success and profitability. Therefore, it is essential for businesses to prioritize ethics and integrate them into their core values and operations.

Corporate social responsibility

Corporate Social Responsibility (CSR) is a concept that describes a company's commitment to behave ethically, contribute to sustainable economic development, and improve the quality of life of its employees, customers, and society at large. CSR is becoming increasingly important for businesses as they seek to build trust and credibility with their stakeholders, including investors, employees, customers, and the wider community. This chapter will explore the principles of corporate social responsibility, the benefits of CSR, and the challenges and criticisms of the concept.

Principles of Corporate Social Responsibility:

The principles of corporate social responsibility are based on the idea that businesses have a responsibility to operate in a way that benefits society as a whole. These principles include the following:

1. Legal and Ethical Behavior: Businesses must comply with all relevant laws and regulations and act in an ethical and responsible manner.

2. Environmental Stewardship: Companies should act in a way that minimizes their impact on the environment and promotes sustainability.

3. Social Responsibility: Companies have a responsibility to respect human rights, support diversity and inclusion, and contribute to the well-being of the communities in which they operate.

4. Transparency and Accountability: Businesses must be transparent about their activities and accountable for their actions, including their impact on the environment and society.

Benefits of Corporate Social Responsibility:

There are several benefits of corporate social responsibility, both for the company and for society as a whole. These include:

1. Improved Reputation: Companies that engage in CSR are often viewed more positively by their stakeholders, which can improve their reputation and help attract and retain customers, employees, and investors.

2. Increased Employee Engagement: Employees are often more engaged and committed to their work when they feel that their employer is committed to making a positive impact on society.

3. Enhanced Customer Loyalty: Customers are often more loyal to companies that demonstrate a commitment to social responsibility.

4. Better Risk Management: Companies that are proactive in managing their social and environmental impact are often better equipped to manage risks and avoid negative consequences.

Challenges and Criticisms of Corporate Social Responsibility:

While CSR has many benefits, it also faces several challenges and criticisms. These include:

1. Cost: Implementing CSR initiatives can be expensive, especially for small and medium-sized businesses.

2. Lack of Consistency: There is often a lack of consistency in how CSR is defined and implemented, which can make it difficult to compare companies' efforts.

3. Greenwashing: Some companies engage in "greenwashing," where they make exaggerated or misleading claims about their environmental or social impact to improve their reputation.

4. Focus on Short-term Gains: Some companies may prioritize short-term gains over long-term sustainability, which can undermine the effectiveness of CSR initiatives.

Conclusion:

Corporate social responsibility is a vital component of modern business practice. Companies that adopt CSR principles and practices can improve their reputation, attract and retain customers and employees, and manage risk more effectively. However, implementing CSR initiatives can be challenging and costly, and there are concerns about the lack of consistency in how CSR is defined and implemented. Despite these challenges, the benefits of CSR make it an essential aspect of business in the 21st century.

Stakeholder theory

Stakeholder theory is a normative theory of business ethics that suggests that businesses have a responsibility to consider the interests of all their stakeholders, rather than just their shareholders. The theory argues that businesses should not just focus on maximizing profits, but also consider the impacts of their decisions on their employees, customers, suppliers, the environment, and the wider community.

Historical Context The origins of stakeholder theory can be traced back to the 1930s and 1940s, when business leaders and academics began to recognize the importance of considering the interests of employees and customers in addition to shareholders. However, it was not until the 1980s that stakeholder theory emerged as a distinct approach to business ethics, largely due to the work of R. Edward Freeman, a business professor at the University of Virginia.

Stakeholder theory gained momentum in the wake of high-profile corporate scandals, such as Enron and WorldCom, which highlighted the need for businesses to take a more ethical and socially responsible approach. The theory has since become increasingly influential, and is now widely used by businesses, policymakers, and academics to guide their decision-making.

Stakeholders Stakeholder theory identifies a range of stakeholders that businesses should consider when making decisions, including:

1. Shareholders: These are the owners of the business, who have a financial interest in its success.

2. Employees: These are the people who work for the business, and whose well-being and interests should be taken into account.

3. Customers: These are the people who buy the business's products or services, and whose needs and preferences should be considered.

4. Suppliers: These are the businesses that provide the goods and services that the business needs to operate, and whose interests should be taken into account.

5. Communities: These are the people who live and work in the areas where the business operates, and whose social and environmental interests should be considered.

6. Government: These are the regulatory bodies and policymakers that oversee and regulate the business, and whose laws and regulations the business must comply with.

7. Environment: These are the natural resources and ecosystems that the business relies on, and whose health and well-being should be taken into account.

Principles of Stakeholder Theory Stakeholder theory is based on several key principles, including:

1. Stakeholders have a legitimate interest in the business's decisions and actions.

2. Businesses should take a holistic approach to decision-making, considering the interests of all stakeholders.

3. Businesses should aim to create long-term value for all stakeholders, rather than just maximizing short-term profits for shareholders.

4. Businesses should be transparent and accountable to their stakeholders, and should communicate openly and honestly with them.

5. Businesses should act in an ethical and socially responsible manner, and should seek to minimize their negative impacts on stakeholders.

Critiques of Stakeholder Theory Despite its widespread use and influence, stakeholder theory has also faced criticism from some quarters. One of the main critiques is that it is too vague and lacks clear guidance on how businesses should balance the interests of different stakeholders. Some argue that the theory is too idealistic and unrealistic, and that businesses cannot realistically prioritize the interests of all stakeholders equally.

Others argue that the theory is too focused on the social and ethical responsibilities of businesses, and does not pay enough attention to their economic responsibilities. Critics also argue that stakeholder theory can be used as a way for businesses to avoid accountability and justify their actions, rather than as a genuine commitment to ethical and responsible behavior.

Conclusion Stakeholder theory is a normative theory of business ethics that argues that businesses have a responsibility to consider the interests of all their stakeholders, rather than just their shareholders. The theory has gained traction in recent years, and is now widely used by businesses, policymakers, and academics to guide their decision-making processes. While there are some criticisms of the theory, such as the difficulty in determining which stakeholders to prioritize, it remains a powerful tool for promoting ethical behavior in business. By recognizing the importance of stakeholders beyond just shareholders, businesses can build stronger relationships with their communities, employees, and customers, leading to long-term success and sustainability. Overall, the adoption of stakeholder theory can lead to more ethical, responsible, and socially-conscious business practices that benefit everyone involved.

Ethical decision making

Introduction: Ethical decision-making is a process that involves identifying, evaluating, and choosing among alternative actions in a way that is consistent with ethical principles and values. Ethical decision-making is an essential component of business ethics, as it helps individuals and organizations navigate complex moral dilemmas that arise in the course of conducting business. In this section, we will discuss the process of ethical decision-making, the various ethical frameworks that can be used to guide decision-making, and the role of organizational culture in promoting ethical behavior.

The process of ethical decision-making: Ethical decision-making is a process that typically involves several steps. The first step is to identify the ethical issue or dilemma. This may involve recognizing that there is a conflict between two or more values or principles, or recognizing that a decision may have negative consequences for one or more stakeholders. The next step is to gather relevant information about the situation, including the potential consequences of different courses of action and the rights and interests of different stakeholders. Once this information has been gathered, it is important to evaluate it in light of ethical principles and values. This may involve considering the ethical frameworks that can be used to guide decision-making, such as utilitarianism, deontology, and virtue ethics. Finally, after evaluating the options, a decision must be made, and the appropriate actions taken.

Ethical frameworks: There are several ethical frameworks that can be used to guide ethical decision-making. One of the most widely used is utilitarianism, which holds that the best course of action is the one that maximizes overall happiness or utility for the greatest number of people. Another framework is deontology, which focuses on the inherent morality of actions, rather than their consequences. Deontological theories hold that certain actions are inherently right or wrong, regardless of their consequences. A third framework is virtue ethics, which emphasizes the character of the individual making the decision, and the importance of developing virtuous character traits such as honesty, compassion, and fairness.

Organizational culture: Organizational culture plays a critical role in promoting ethical behavior in the workplace. A positive organizational culture is one that promotes ethical behavior and holds employees accountable for their actions. Organizations can promote ethical behavior by providing employees with training and resources that help them make ethical decisions, by setting clear expectations for ethical behavior, and by creating an environment in which employees feel comfortable raising ethical concerns. Organizations can also promote ethical behavior by establishing a code of conduct that outlines the organization's values and principles, and by enforcing this code of conduct consistently and fairly.

Conclusion: Ethical decision-making is a complex process that involves identifying ethical issues, evaluating options, and making decisions that are consistent with ethical principles and values. There are several ethical frameworks that can be used to guide decision-making, including utilitarianism, deontology, and virtue ethics. Organizational culture plays a critical role in promoting ethical behavior in the workplace, and organizations can promote ethical behavior by providing training and resources, setting clear expectations, and creating an environment in which employees feel comfortable raising ethical concerns. Ultimately, ethical decision-making is essential for building trust, promoting accountability, and maintaining the integrity of the business community.

Whistleblowing

Whistleblowing is the act of exposing wrongdoing or illegal activities within an organization or institution. It involves an individual, usually an employee, speaking out against illegal or unethical behavior within their workplace, often at great personal risk. Whistleblowers are typically motivated by a desire to uphold their own moral and ethical standards, and to protect the interests of others, such as co-workers, customers, or the general public.

Whistleblowing can take many forms, ranging from internal reporting to external disclosure to the media or government authorities. In recent years, the role of whistleblowers in exposing corporate wrongdoing has become increasingly important, especially in light of high-profile cases such as the Enron scandal and the global financial crisis.

While whistleblowers can play a vital role in exposing corporate misconduct, they often face significant personal and professional risks as a result of their actions. These risks can include termination of employment, blacklisting in their industry, and even physical harm in extreme cases. Therefore, it is important for whistleblowers to be aware of their legal rights and protections, as well as the potential consequences of their actions.

One of the key ethical issues surrounding whistleblowing is the tension between loyalty to one's employer and loyalty to society as a whole. Many people feel a sense of loyalty or obligation to their employer, and may be reluctant to speak out against them for fear of retribution or other negative consequences. However, others argue that in cases of serious wrongdoing, such as fraud or corruption, the interests of society as a whole should take precedence over the interests of any individual or organization.

Another ethical issue surrounding whistleblowing is the question of when it is appropriate to blow the whistle. Some argue that whistleblowing should be a last resort, and that employees should first try to address any concerns through internal channels, such as reporting to a supervisor or the company's ethics hotline. Others argue that if internal channels have failed or are not available, whistleblowers have a moral obligation to speak out to external authorities, such as the media or government agencies.

In addition to legal and ethical considerations, whistleblowers may also face practical challenges in terms of how to blow the whistle effectively. For example, whistleblowers may need to gather and present evidence in order to support their claims, which can be difficult or risky to do without proper resources or support. Additionally, whistleblowers may face challenges in terms of how to navigate media attention or public scrutiny, especially if their allegations are controversial or disputed.

Overall, whistleblowing is an important and complex ethical issue that requires careful consideration of the potential risks, benefits, and ethical implications. While whistleblowers can play a crucial role in exposing corporate misconduct and promoting accountability, they also face significant personal and professional risks as a result of their actions. Therefore, it is important for individuals and organizations to be aware of their legal and ethical obligations regarding whistleblowing, and to provide support and protections for those who speak out against wrongdoing.

Fair trade

Fair trade is an economic system that seeks to ensure that workers and producers in developing countries receive fair prices and working conditions for their products. The movement began in the 1940s and has since grown to become an important force in the global economy. Fair trade is often contrasted with conventional trade, which is characterized by a lack of transparency and accountability, as well as exploitative practices such as child labor and unsafe working conditions. This article will explore the concept of fair trade, its principles, and the impact it has had on the global economy.

Principles of Fair Trade:

There are several principles that guide fair trade practices. The first is fair prices for products. Fair trade organizations work to ensure that producers receive prices that cover the costs of sustainable production, as well as a premium that can be invested in community development. This helps to ensure that workers and producers can earn a living wage and invest in their communities.

The second principle is fair labor conditions. Fair trade organizations require that workers are treated fairly and have access to safe working conditions. They also prohibit child labor and discrimination against women and minorities. This helps to ensure that workers are able to earn a living wage and that their rights are protected.

The third principle is environmental sustainability. Fair trade organizations work to promote sustainable farming practices and reduce the use of harmful pesticides and fertilizers. This helps to protect the environment and ensure that future generations have access to natural resources.

Impact of Fair Trade:

Fair trade has had a significant impact on the global economy. According to the Fairtrade Foundation, in 2020, more than 1.6 million farmers and workers in 73 countries were part of the fair trade system. Fair trade sales amounted to $9.4 billion, a significant increase from previous years.

One of the key benefits of fair trade is that it helps to reduce poverty and promote economic development in developing countries. Fair trade organizations work with small-scale producers and farmers, who often struggle to compete in the global market. By providing fair prices and access to new markets, fair trade helps to empower these communities and create economic opportunities.

Another benefit of fair trade is that it promotes environmental sustainability. Fair trade organizations work to promote sustainable farming practices and reduce the use of harmful pesticides and fertilizers. This helps to protect the environment and ensure that natural resources are preserved for future generations.

Challenges and Criticisms:

While fair trade has had many positive impacts, it is not without its challenges and criticisms. One of the main criticisms of fair trade is that it is not scalable. Fair trade often focuses on small-scale producers and farmers, which limits its impact on the global economy. Additionally, some critics argue that fair trade products are often more expensive than conventional products, which limits their appeal to consumers.

Another challenge is that fair trade is often criticized for being too bureaucratic and expensive. Some fair trade organizations require extensive documentation and certification processes, which can be difficult and expensive for small-scale producers and farmers to navigate. Additionally, fair trade products often require higher production costs, which can make them less competitive in the global market.

Conclusion:

Fair trade is an important movement that seeks to promote economic development, environmental sustainability, and social justice. By providing fair prices, promoting sustainable farming practices, and supporting small-scale producers and farmers, fair trade has had a significant impact on the global economy. While there are challenges and criticisms of fair trade, it is clear that the movement has the potential to create positive change in the world.

Chapter 8: Data Analysis

Principles of data analysis

Introduction: Data analysis is the process of examining and interpreting data with the aim of gaining useful insights and making informed decisions. It involves the application of various statistical and mathematical techniques to identify patterns, trends, and relationships within the data. Principles of data analysis provide a framework for conducting effective data analysis. In this article, we will discuss the fundamental principles of data analysis that are critical for obtaining reliable and accurate results.

Principles of Data Analysis:

1. Clearly Define the Research Question: The first principle of data analysis is to have a clear understanding of the research question. This involves defining the problem that needs to be solved and formulating a specific research question. Having a well-defined research question is essential as it guides the entire data analysis process and helps to ensure that the analysis is relevant and focused.

2. Choose the Appropriate Methodology: There are many different data analysis methodologies available, and it is crucial to choose the appropriate methodology for the research question. The methodology should be selected based on the type of data, the research question, and the objectives of the analysis. Choosing the right methodology ensures that the analysis is valid and reliable.

3. Ensure Data Quality: The quality of data used for analysis is crucial. The data should be reliable, accurate, and relevant. Before conducting any analysis, it is essential to assess the quality of the data and ensure that it is appropriate for the research question. The data should also be cleaned and prepared to eliminate any errors or inconsistencies.

4. Analyze Data Appropriately: The analysis of data should be appropriate to the research question and the data collected. This involves selecting the appropriate statistical techniques, data visualizations, and data modeling methods. The analysis should be conducted systematically and rigorously to ensure that the results are reliable and valid.

5. Interpret the Results: Once the data analysis is completed, it is essential to interpret the results. The interpretation should be done in a way that is relevant to the research question and should take into account any limitations of the data or analysis. The interpretation should be presented in a clear and concise manner, using appropriate visualizations or tables.

6. Communicate Findings Effectively: The final principle of data analysis is to communicate the findings effectively. This involves presenting the results in a way that is easily understood by the intended audience. The findings should be presented in a clear and concise manner, using appropriate visualizations, tables, or graphs. It is also essential to provide a

context for the findings and to highlight any implications or recommendations for future research or practice.

Conclusion: Data analysis is an essential process in many fields, including business, science, and social sciences. The principles of data analysis discussed in this article provide a framework for conducting effective and reliable data analysis. By following these principles, researchers can ensure that their data analysis is rigorous, valid, and relevant to the research question.

Statistical analysis

Statistical analysis is a fundamental tool in data analysis that involves the application of statistical methods to collect, analyze, and interpret data. It allows researchers to make sense of large amounts of data and to draw conclusions from that data. Statistical analysis is used in many fields, including business, economics, social sciences, and healthcare, to name a few. In this section, we will discuss some of the most commonly used statistical techniques.

Descriptive Statistics: Descriptive statistics are used to describe the characteristics of a dataset. They include measures of central tendency, such as the mean, median, and mode, as well as measures of variability, such as the range, standard deviation, and variance. These statistics help researchers to understand the distribution of the data and to identify any outliers or unusual values.

Inferential Statistics: Inferential statistics are used to make inferences about a population based on a sample of data. They involve hypothesis testing and the use of confidence intervals. Hypothesis testing involves comparing a sample to a known population parameter and determining the probability that the sample is representative of the population. Confidence intervals are used to estimate the range of values in which the true population parameter is likely to fall.

Regression Analysis: Regression analysis is a statistical technique used to establish the relationship between two or more variables. It is commonly used in business and economics to predict future outcomes based on historical data. Regression analysis involves fitting a line or curve to the data and determining the strength and direction of the relationship between the variables.

Time-Series Analysis: Time-series analysis is a statistical technique used to analyze data that is collected over time. It involves examining patterns in the data, such as trends and seasonality, and making predictions about future values based on historical data. Time-series analysis is used in many fields, including finance, economics, and environmental studies.

Data Mining: Data mining is the process of discovering patterns and relationships in large datasets. It involves using statistical and machine learning techniques to identify trends and patterns that are not immediately apparent. Data mining is used in many fields, including marketing, healthcare, and finance.

Cluster Analysis: Cluster analysis is a statistical technique used to group data points based on similarities or differences. It involves identifying clusters of data points that are close together in terms of their characteristics and grouping them together. Cluster analysis is used in many fields, including marketing, genetics, and social sciences.

Conclusion: Statistical analysis is an essential tool in data analysis that allows researchers to make sense of large amounts of data and to draw conclusions from that data. It involves the use of statistical techniques such as descriptive statistics, inferential statistics, regression analysis, time-series analysis, data mining, and cluster analysis. These techniques are used in many fields, including business, economics, social sciences, and healthcare, to name a few. By using statistical analysis, researchers can make informed decisions based on data-driven insights.

Regression analysis" the sub topic for about 3000 words long

Regression analysis is a statistical technique that is commonly used in data analysis to identify and quantify the relationship between a dependent variable and one or more independent variables. The dependent variable is the outcome variable, and the independent variables are the predictor variables that are believed to influence the outcome variable.

There are several types of regression analysis, including linear regression, multiple regression, logistic regression, and nonlinear regression. Linear regression is the simplest type and is used when the relationship between the dependent and independent variables is assumed to be linear. Multiple regression is used when there are multiple independent variables, and logistic regression is used when the dependent variable is categorical.

The process of performing a regression analysis involves several steps. The first step is to collect the data and identify the dependent variable and independent variables. The next step is to plot the data to visualize the relationship between the variables. If the relationship appears to be linear, a linear regression model can be used.

The linear regression model involves calculating the slope and intercept of the line that best fits the data. The slope represents the change in the dependent variable for every one-unit change in the independent variable, and the intercept represents the value of the dependent variable when the independent variable is zero.

Once the model is fitted, it is important to assess its goodness of fit. This can be done by calculating the coefficient of determination (R-squared), which represents the proportion of variance in the dependent variable that can be explained by the independent variable(s). A value of R-squared close to 1 indicates a good fit, while a value close to 0 indicates a poor fit.

Regression analysis has many practical applications in business and economics. For example, it can be used to predict sales based on advertising expenditure, to estimate the impact of price changes on demand, or to determine the relationship between employee productivity and training.

However, it is important to remember that regression analysis is not a causal technique, and correlation does not imply causation. It is also important to ensure that the assumptions of the regression model are met, such as the independence of observations and the normality of residuals.

In conclusion, regression analysis is a powerful statistical technique that can help businesses and economists understand and predict the relationships between variables. It is a useful tool for making data-driven decisions and can provide valuable insights into business operations. However, it is important to use regression analysis with caution and to ensure that the assumptions of the model are met.

Forecasting

Introduction: Forecasting is an essential component of data analysis and decision-making processes in various industries. Forecasting involves predicting future trends and values based on past data, and it is used in a wide range of applications, from weather forecasting to financial forecasting. In this section, we will discuss the principles and techniques of forecasting, including time series analysis, trend analysis, and regression analysis.

Time Series Analysis: Time series analysis is a statistical technique used to analyze and interpret time-based data. Time series data involves measuring the same variable at different points in time. Time series data can be analyzed to identify trends, seasonal patterns, and other patterns that may be present in the data. Time series analysis involves four basic components: trend, seasonality, cyclical patterns, and random variation. Trend refers to the long-term direction of the data. Seasonality refers to the pattern of data that repeats over a fixed period, such as a year or a quarter. Cyclical patterns refer to the fluctuation of data over a longer period of time, such as a business cycle. Random variation refers to the unpredictable fluctuations in the data.

Trend Analysis: Trend analysis is a method used to analyze time series data to identify and measure trends in the data. Trend analysis involves plotting the data points on a graph and then fitting a line or curve to the data points. The slope of the line or curve indicates the direction and strength of the trend. Positive slopes indicate an upward trend, while negative slopes indicate a downward trend. Trend analysis can be used to forecast future values of the variable based on the trend identified in the data.

Regression Analysis: Regression analysis is a statistical technique used to analyze the relationship between two or more variables. Regression analysis involves fitting a regression line to the data and then using the line to predict the values of the dependent variable based on the values of the independent variable(s). Regression analysis can be used for forecasting purposes, as it can help predict future values of the dependent variable based on the values of the independent variable(s). There are various types of regression analysis, including linear regression, multiple regression, and logistic regression.

Forecasting Techniques: There are various forecasting techniques used in data analysis, including time series analysis, trend analysis, and regression analysis. Other forecasting techniques include exponential smoothing, moving averages, and neural networks. Exponential smoothing is a technique used to analyze time series data by smoothing out the fluctuations in the data. Moving averages involve averaging out the values of the data over a fixed period to identify trends and patterns. Neural networks involve training a computer model to recognize patterns in the data and make predictions based on those patterns.

Conclusion: Forecasting is an essential component of data analysis and decision-making processes in various industries. Time series analysis, trend analysis, and regression analysis are commonly used forecasting techniques that can help predict future trends and values based on past data. Other forecasting techniques, such as exponential smoothing, moving averages, and neural networks, are also used to analyze and interpret data. By understanding and applying these principles and techniques of forecasting, businesses can make more informed decisions and improve their operations and profitability.

Big data, including blockchain and cryptocurrency transaction data

Introduction: Big data is a term used to describe the massive volume of structured and unstructured data that is generated by individuals, organizations, and devices. This data is too large and complex to be processed using traditional data processing techniques, and requires specialized tools and techniques to extract insights and value. In recent years, blockchain and cryptocurrency transaction data have emerged as important sources of big data, presenting unique challenges and opportunities for analysis.

What is Blockchain Technology? Blockchain technology is a decentralized, distributed ledger that records transactions on multiple computers in a secure, transparent, and tamper-proof manner. Each transaction is verified by a network of nodes before it is added to the blockchain, and once recorded, cannot be altered or deleted without consensus from the network. This makes blockchain data an attractive source of big data for analysis, as it is secure and reliable, and can be used to track the movement of assets, goods, and services in real-time.

What are Cryptocurrencies? Cryptocurrencies are digital or virtual tokens that use cryptography to secure and verify transactions, and to control the creation of new units. Unlike traditional currencies, cryptocurrencies are not issued by a central authority, and their value is determined by supply and demand in the market. Cryptocurrency transactions are recorded on a blockchain, and can be used to track the movement of funds, as well as to conduct anonymous transactions.

Challenges and Opportunities of Analyzing Blockchain and Cryptocurrency Transaction Data: Analyzing blockchain and cryptocurrency transaction data presents several unique challenges, including the need to access and process large volumes of data in real-time, the need to identify and classify transactions accurately, and the need to ensure the security and privacy of sensitive data. However, it also presents several opportunities for analysis, including the ability to track the movement of assets and funds, to detect and prevent fraud and money laundering, and to identify patterns and trends in market behavior.

Tools and Techniques for Analyzing Blockchain and Cryptocurrency Transaction Data: There are several tools and techniques that can be used to analyze blockchain and cryptocurrency transaction data, including data visualization, machine learning, and natural language processing. Data visualization can be used to create visual representations of transaction data, allowing analysts to identify patterns and trends quickly and easily. Machine learning can be used to develop predictive models and algorithms that can detect anomalies and patterns in transaction data. Natural language processing can be used to analyze text data related to cryptocurrencies, such as social media posts and news articles.

Applications of Blockchain and Cryptocurrency Transaction Data Analysis: There are several applications of blockchain and cryptocurrency transaction data analysis, including fraud detection and prevention, market analysis and forecasting, and compliance and regulatory reporting. Fraud detection and prevention can be achieved by analyzing transaction data to identify suspicious patterns and behavior, such as large transfers to unknown accounts or unusual trading activity. Market analysis and forecasting can be achieved by analyzing transaction data to identify trends and patterns in market behavior, such as the correlation between trading volume and price movements. Compliance and regulatory reporting can be achieved by analyzing transaction data to ensure that transactions comply with relevant laws and regulations.

Conclusion: In conclusion, blockchain and cryptocurrency transaction data present unique challenges and opportunities for analysis, requiring specialized tools and techniques to extract insights and value. Analyzing this data can be used to detect and prevent fraud, to identify patterns and trends in market behavior, and to ensure compliance and regulatory reporting. As blockchain and cryptocurrency adoption continues to grow, the importance of analyzing this data will only increase, making it an important area of study for analysts and researchers alike.

Data visualization

Data visualization is the representation of data and information in a visual format such as graphs, charts, and maps to help users understand complex information and relationships quickly. It is an essential tool in data analysis that enables analysts to identify patterns and trends and communicate insights effectively. In this section, we will discuss the importance of data visualization, different types of data visualization, and best practices for creating effective visualizations.

Importance of Data Visualization: Data visualization plays a crucial role in the data analysis process as it allows users to:

1. Identify patterns and trends: Data visualization makes it easier to identify patterns, trends, and relationships in data that would otherwise be challenging to discover.

2. Communicate insights effectively: Visuals are much easier to understand than raw data, especially when dealing with large datasets. Visualization makes it possible to communicate insights effectively and efficiently.

3. Make data-driven decisions: Visualization enables decision-makers to see the data in a new light, providing a better understanding of the situation, and enabling them to make informed decisions.

Types of Data Visualization: There are several types of data visualization, including:

1. Line charts: A line chart is a graphical representation of data that shows the relationship between two or more variables over time.

2. Bar charts: A bar chart is a graphical representation of data that uses bars of different heights to represent different quantities or values.

3. Pie charts: A pie chart is a graphical representation of data that uses a circle divided into slices to represent different quantities or values.

4. Scatter plots: A scatter plot is a graphical representation of data that shows the relationship between two or more variables.

5. Heat maps: A heat map is a graphical representation of data that uses color to represent different values in a matrix or table.

6. Tree maps: A tree map is a graphical representation of data that uses nested rectangles to represent data hierarchies.

Best Practices for Creating Effective Visualizations: To create effective visualizations, analysts should consider the following best practices:

1. Understand your audience: Before creating a visualization, it's essential to understand your audience and their needs to create visuals that are relevant to them.

2. Choose the right chart type: Choosing the right chart type is essential to create an effective visualization that accurately represents the data.

3. Keep it simple: Avoid cluttering the visualization with too many data points or unnecessary information, and keep it simple and easy to understand.

4. Use color effectively: Color can be an effective tool to highlight data points or trends, but it's essential to use it sparingly and consistently.

5. Label your visuals: Always label your visualizations to help users understand what they are looking at and provide context for the data.

In conclusion, data visualization is a critical tool in data analysis that enables analysts to identify patterns and trends, communicate insights effectively, and make data-driven decisions. By choosing the right visualization type, following best practices, and using the right tools, analysts can create effective visualizations that communicate insights clearly and help decision-makers understand complex data quickly.

Healthcare

Healthcare Case Study: Improving Patient Outcomes through Technology and Data Analysis

Introduction: The healthcare industry is constantly evolving, and the adoption of technology has played a significant role in transforming patient outcomes. With the increasing availability of health data, providers are leveraging data analysis tools and techniques to improve clinical outcomes and patient experiences. This case study will explore how a healthcare provider successfully implemented a data analysis platform to improve patient outcomes and reduce healthcare costs.

Background: Our case study focuses on a large hospital system that serves a diverse patient population across multiple locations. The hospital system was facing several challenges, including high healthcare costs, variability in clinical outcomes, and difficulty in managing patient data effectively. The healthcare provider recognized the need for a data analysis platform that could provide real-time insights into patient outcomes and improve clinical decision-making.

Strategy: The healthcare provider developed a data analysis platform that integrated clinical data from electronic health records, financial data, and patient satisfaction data. The platform used data visualization techniques to present real-time insights into patient outcomes, including length of stay, readmission rates, and patient satisfaction scores. The healthcare provider also employed a team of data analysts to monitor the platform and provide insights to clinical teams.

Implementation: The healthcare provider implemented the data analysis platform across all its locations, training clinical staff and administrators to use the platform effectively. The platform provided real-time feedback to clinical teams, enabling them to identify areas for improvement in patient care and make informed decisions about treatment plans. The platform also helped clinical teams to identify patients who were at high risk for readmission and develop personalized care plans to reduce the risk of readmission.

Results: The healthcare provider saw significant improvements in patient outcomes following the implementation of the data analysis platform. The platform helped reduce readmission rates by 20%, improve patient satisfaction scores by 15%, and decrease the length of stay by 10%. The platform also helped the hospital system reduce healthcare costs by optimizing patient care plans and reducing the need for costly interventions.

Conclusion: The healthcare industry is undergoing a significant transformation, and the adoption of technology and data analysis is driving improvements in patient outcomes and reducing healthcare costs. Our case study demonstrated how a healthcare provider successfully implemented a data analysis platform to improve patient outcomes and reduce healthcare costs. As healthcare providers continue to adopt data analysis tools and techniques, patients can expect to receive better quality care and a more personalized healthcare experience.

Technology, including blockchain and digital assets

Introduction: Technology has been one of the fastest-growing sectors in recent years, with new innovations emerging every day. Blockchain, a distributed ledger technology that enables secure and transparent transactions, is one such innovation that has disrupted several industries, including finance and supply chain management. Digital assets, which are digital representations of value, are also gaining popularity as a means of investment and exchange. This case study explores the use of blockchain and digital assets in various industries and their potential impact on the future of business.

Overview of Blockchain and Digital Assets: Blockchain is a decentralized and immutable digital ledger that records transactions in a secure and transparent manner. It allows for peer-to-peer transactions without the need for intermediaries, thereby reducing transaction costs and increasing efficiency. Digital assets, on the other hand, are digital representations of value that can be transferred and traded electronically. They include cryptocurrencies, digital tokens, and other blockchain-based assets.

Use of Blockchain and Digital Assets in Finance: Blockchain and digital assets have disrupted the traditional financial industry by enabling faster and more secure transactions. Cryptocurrencies, such as Bitcoin and Ethereum, have gained popularity as alternative means of payment and investment. Digital tokens, which represent ownership in a particular asset, have also been used for fundraising through initial coin offerings (ICOs). Blockchain technology has also been used for trade finance, cross-border payments, and asset management.

Use of Blockchain and Digital Assets in Supply Chain Management: Blockchain technology has the potential to transform supply chain management by enabling greater transparency and traceability. It allows for the tracking of goods and materials from the point of origin to the point of consumption, thereby reducing the risk of fraud and counterfeiting. Digital tokens can also be used to represent ownership of physical assets, such as commodities and real estate, and enable fractional ownership and trading.

Challenges and Risks: Despite the potential benefits of blockchain and digital assets, there are also several challenges and risks associated with their use. One of the main challenges is the lack of standardization and regulation, which can lead to uncertainty and volatility in the market. Security and privacy concerns, such as the risk of hacking and theft, are also major risks associated with digital assets. Additionally, the energy consumption required for blockchain-based transactions is a growing concern for environmental sustainability.

Future Outlook: Blockchain and digital assets are still in the early stages of development, and their potential impact on the future of business is yet to be fully realized. However, the growing interest and investment in these technologies suggest that they are here to stay. As more businesses and industries adopt blockchain and digital assets, there is a need for standardization and regulation to ensure their safe and secure use.

Conclusion: Blockchain and digital assets are disruptive technologies that have the potential to transform several industries, including finance and supply chain management. While there are challenges and risks associated with their use, the growing interest and investment in these technologies suggest that they are here to stay. As businesses and industries continue to adopt blockchain and digital assets, it is important to ensure their safe and secure use through standardization and regulation.

Energy and environment

The energy sector has become increasingly important in recent years due to concerns about climate change and the need for more sustainable sources of energy. The environment has also become a critical issue, with the public demanding that businesses take action to reduce their impact on the environment. This chapter will examine case studies in the energy and environment sectors to highlight the challenges and opportunities facing businesses in these areas.

Case Study 1: Tesla

Tesla is a company that designs and manufactures electric cars, energy storage systems, and solar products. The company's mission is to accelerate the transition to sustainable energy. Tesla's success can be attributed to its innovative approach to product design, as well as its focus on sustainability.

One of the key challenges facing Tesla is the high cost of its products. The company's cars and energy storage systems are expensive, which limits their appeal to a niche market. Tesla is addressing this challenge by investing in research and development to reduce costs and increase efficiency. The company is also working to expand its product line to appeal to a wider audience.

Another challenge facing Tesla is the lack of infrastructure for electric vehicles. In many areas, there are few charging stations, which limits the range of electric cars. Tesla is addressing this challenge by investing in its Supercharger network, which provides fast charging for its vehicles.

Tesla has also faced criticism for its environmental impact. The company's production process consumes a significant amount of energy, and its battery production generates hazardous waste. Tesla is addressing these concerns by investing in renewable energy and developing new battery recycling technologies.

Case Study 2: BP

BP is a multinational oil and gas company that has faced significant challenges in recent years. The company's reputation was damaged by the Deepwater Horizon oil spill in 2010, which resulted in significant environmental damage and a loss of life. BP has since committed to improving its environmental performance and reducing its carbon footprint.

One of the key challenges facing BP is the transition to a low-carbon economy. The company's core business is oil and gas production, which is a significant contributor to greenhouse gas emissions. BP is addressing this challenge by investing in renewable energy and exploring new technologies to reduce emissions.

Another challenge facing BP is the need to improve safety and reliability. The Deepwater Horizon disaster highlighted the importance of safety and the need for robust risk management systems. BP has since implemented a range of measures to improve safety, including enhanced training for employees and improved safety procedures.

BP has also faced criticism for its involvement in controversial projects, such as the Canadian oil sands. The company is addressing these concerns by reviewing its portfolio and divesting from high-carbon assets.

Conclusion:

The energy and environment sectors present significant challenges and opportunities for businesses. Companies that are able to innovate and develop sustainable solutions will be well-positioned to succeed in these sectors. However, businesses must also be mindful of their impact on the environment and work to reduce their carbon footprint. The case studies of Tesla and BP highlight the importance of innovation, safety, and sustainability in the energy and environment sectors.

Education

Introduction Education is a fundamental pillar of society, providing individuals with knowledge, skills, and values that enable them to lead fulfilling lives and contribute to the development of their communities. This chapter explores case studies that illustrate how innovative approaches to education can address pressing challenges and drive positive change. The cases range from K-12 education to higher education and lifelong learning.

Case 1: Digital Learning Platforms in K-12 Education Digital learning platforms have transformed the way students and teachers engage with educational content. In many cases, these platforms have made learning more interactive and personalized, allowing students to progress at their own pace and access a wealth of resources beyond traditional textbooks. One example is the Khan Academy, which offers free online courses and instructional videos on a wide range of subjects. Another example is ClassDojo, a communication platform that enables teachers and parents to share updates and feedback on students' progress.

Case 2: Blended Learning in Higher Education Blended learning is an approach that combines online and face-to-face instruction to create a more flexible and interactive learning experience. This approach has gained popularity in higher education as universities seek to meet the needs of a diverse student body and adapt to changing technologies. One example is Arizona State University's Global Freshman Academy, which offers students the opportunity to earn college credit through online courses that are both self-paced and instructor-led. Another example is Harvard Business School's HBX platform, which offers online business courses that incorporate interactive case studies and peer learning.

Case 3: Lifelong Learning for Sustainable Development Lifelong learning is increasingly important in today's rapidly changing economy, where new technologies and industries are constantly emerging. Moreover, lifelong learning is essential for achieving sustainable development, which requires a continuous process of education and training to build knowledge, skills, and values that support environmental, social, and economic well-being. One example is the Sustainable Development Goals Academy, a digital learning platform that offers courses on the United Nations' Sustainable Development Goals. Another example is the Massive Open Online Course (MOOC) platform Coursera, which offers courses on a wide range of subjects, including sustainability and social entrepreneurship.

Conclusion These case studies demonstrate how innovative approaches to education can address pressing challenges and drive positive change. Digital learning platforms, blended learning, and lifelong learning are just a few examples of how education is evolving to meet the needs of a rapidly changing world. As these approaches continue to evolve, it is essential to ensure that they promote equity, inclusivity, and sustainability, and that they prepare learners for the challenges and opportunities of the future.

International development

Introduction: International development refers to the efforts made by different organizations, governments, and individuals to promote the economic, social, and political well-being of people in developing countries. These efforts aim to alleviate poverty, improve access to education, health care, and other basic needs, and promote sustainable development. In this chapter, we will examine some case studies that demonstrate the challenges and opportunities of international development, the different approaches and strategies employed, and the impact of these efforts on the people and communities involved.

Case Study 1: Microfinance in Bangladesh Microfinance is a financial service that provides small loans, savings, and insurance to low-income individuals who lack access to traditional banking services. The concept was pioneered in Bangladesh in the 1970s by Muhammad Yunus and the Grameen Bank. The bank has since disbursed billions of dollars in loans to millions of borrowers, most of whom are women. The loans have been used to start or expand small businesses, improve housing, and pay for education and health care. The success of microfinance in Bangladesh has inspired similar initiatives around the world and has contributed to the reduction of poverty in many countries.

Case Study 2: HIV/AIDS Prevention in Sub-Saharan Africa Sub-Saharan Africa has been hit hard by the HIV/AIDS epidemic, which has led to millions of deaths and devastating social and economic consequences. Efforts to prevent the spread of the disease have involved a range of approaches, including education, counseling, testing, and treatment. One notable initiative is the President's Emergency Plan for AIDS Relief (PEPFAR), launched by the U.S. government in 2003. The program has provided billions of dollars in funding to support prevention, care, and treatment services in more than 50 countries. It has helped to increase access to antiretroviral therapy, reduce the number of new infections, and improve the quality of life for people living with HIV/AIDS.

Case Study 3: Sustainable Agriculture in Peru Agriculture is a critical sector in many developing countries, providing food and livelihoods for millions of people. However, traditional farming practices often involve the use of chemicals that can harm the environment and human health, and can be expensive for small-scale farmers. The Sustainable Agriculture and Rural Development (SARD) program, implemented in Peru by the International Fund for Agricultural Development (IFAD), aims to promote environmentally sustainable and socially inclusive agriculture practices. The program provides training, technical assistance, and financial support to farmers to help them adopt practices such as crop diversification, soil conservation, and organic farming. The program has helped to improve the productivity and income of farmers, while also reducing the negative environmental impacts of agriculture.

Case Study 4: Education in Rwanda Rwanda is a country that has made significant progress in improving access to education, especially at the primary level. In 2003, the government launched the nine-year Basic Education program, which made primary education free and compulsory. The program has led to a significant increase in the number of children enrolled in school and has helped to reduce the gender gap in education. However, the quality of education remains a challenge, with many schools lacking basic resources such as textbooks and qualified teachers. To address this issue, the government has implemented a range of initiatives, including teacher training, curriculum reform, and the use of technology to improve access to educational materials.

Conclusion: International development is a complex and multifaceted field that requires a coordinated and holistic approach to address the challenges facing developing countries. The case studies presented in this chapter demonstrate the importance of partnership, innovation, and sustainability in achieving positive outcomes. The lessons learned from these examples can inform future efforts to promote economic growth, improve social conditions, and promote environmental sustainability in developing countries. Ultimately, international development is a shared responsibility, and requires the commitment and collaboration of governments, non-governmental organizations, businesses, and individuals to make a meaningful impact. By leveraging the expertise and resources of diverse stakeholders, we can work towards building more equitable and prosperous societies for all. It is crucial that we continue to learn from the successes and failures of past development initiatives, and remain committed to promoting sustainable and inclusive development that benefits communities around the world.

Conclusion

Summary of the main points

Throughout this book, we have explored a wide range of topics related to business, technology, and social impact. In this concluding chapter, we will summarize the main points of each chapter, highlighting the key takeaways and insights.

Chapter 1: Introduction In this chapter, we discussed the scope and purpose of the book. We explored the various topics that we would cover, including business ethics, data analysis, case studies, and more. We also highlighted the importance of social impact in today's business landscape and the role of technology in shaping the future.

Chapter 2: Innovation Innovation is a critical driver of growth and progress in today's business environment. This chapter explored the concept of innovation, its importance in business, and the various approaches to fostering innovation. We also discussed the role of technology in driving innovation and highlighted some of the key trends and challenges.

Chapter 3: Entrepreneurship Entrepreneurship is the engine of economic growth, and this chapter explored the various aspects of starting and running a successful business. We discussed the key characteristics of entrepreneurs, the various types of entrepreneurship, and the challenges and opportunities in the entrepreneurial landscape. We also explored the role of technology in supporting entrepreneurship and the importance of social impact in business ventures.

Chapter 4: Marketing and Branding Marketing and branding are critical components of any business strategy, and this chapter explored the various aspects of effective marketing and branding. We discussed the importance of market research, segmentation, and targeting, as well as the role of branding in creating a unique identity and value proposition. We also explored the challenges and opportunities presented by digital marketing and the importance of social impact in building a brand.

Chapter 5: Finance and Investment Finance and investment are critical to the success of any business, and this chapter explored the various aspects of financial management and investment strategies. We discussed the importance of financial planning, budgeting, and forecasting, as well as the role of investors and financial institutions. We also explored the challenges and opportunities presented by emerging financial technologies, such as blockchain and cryptocurrency.

Chapter 6: Technology and Society Technology is rapidly changing the world we live in, and this chapter explored the various ways in which technology is shaping society. We discussed the impact of technology on the economy, the workforce, and society as a whole. We also explored the challenges and opportunities presented by emerging technologies, such as artificial intelligence, the Internet of Things, and blockchain.

Chapter 7: Business Ethics Business ethics are critical to the success and sustainability of any business, and this chapter explored the various aspects of ethical decision-making and corporate social responsibility. We discussed the importance of stakeholder theory, ethical leadership, and fair trade. We also explored the challenges and opportunities presented by whistleblowing and the importance of ethical decision-making in the digital age.

Chapter 8: Data Analysis Data analysis is essential to making informed business decisions, and this chapter explored the various aspects of statistical analysis, regression analysis, forecasting, big data, and data visualization. We discussed the importance of using data to drive decision-making, as well as the challenges and opportunities presented by emerging technologies, such as blockchain and cryptocurrency.

Chapter 9: Case Studies In this chapter, we explored a range of case studies from various industries and sectors, including healthcare, technology, energy and environment, education, and international development. We discussed the key takeaways and insights from each case study, highlighting the importance of innovation, entrepreneurship, marketing and branding, finance and investment, technology and society, and business ethics.

Conclusion: In conclusion, this book has explored a wide range of topics related to business, technology, and social impact. We have discussed the importance of innovation, entrepreneurship, marketing and branding, finance and investment, technology and society, and business ethics. We have also examined various case studies in healthcare, education, energy and environment, international development, and technology, including blockchain and digital assets. Throughout this book, we have highlighted the interconnectivity between these topics, and how businesses can leverage them to create positive social impact while still achieving financial success.

One of the key takeaways from this book is the importance of sustainability in all aspects of business. From product development to supply chain management, sustainability considerations must be integrated into business decisions to ensure long-term success. We have also emphasized the significance of stakeholder theory in guiding ethical decision-making, which involves considering the interests of all stakeholders in business operations, not just shareholders.

Furthermore, we have explored the role of data analysis and visualization in business decision-making, highlighting the importance of utilizing statistical methods and tools to extract meaningful insights from data. We have also discussed the emergence of big data, including blockchain and cryptocurrency transaction data, and the potential opportunities and challenges they present for businesses.

Ultimately, this book has shown that business can be a force for good, creating social impact while still achieving financial success. The case studies presented in this book demonstrate the importance of collaboration, innovation, and sustainability in achieving positive outcomes for businesses and society as a whole. By embracing these principles, businesses can navigate the rapidly changing technological and social landscape and create a better future for all.

Insights into the future of business and economics, including digital assets and blockchain

The world of business and economics is constantly evolving, and there are several key insights into the future of these fields that can be gleaned from recent developments. One of the most important trends to watch is the rise of digital assets and blockchain technology.

Digital assets, also known as cryptocurrencies or virtual currencies, are digital representations of value that are secured by cryptography and operate independently of a central authority. They are increasingly being recognized as a legitimate form of investment and payment, and many experts believe that they will play an important role in the future of the global economy.

Blockchain technology, which underpins many digital assets, is a distributed ledger system that enables secure and transparent transactions without the need for intermediaries. It has the potential to revolutionize the way that businesses and governments operate, and many industries are already exploring its potential uses.

One area where digital assets and blockchain technology are likely to have a significant impact is in the world of finance and investment. Digital assets offer new opportunities for diversification and risk management, and blockchain technology has the potential to reduce costs and increase transparency in financial transactions.

Another area where digital assets and blockchain technology are likely to be important is in supply chain management. The ability to track products and materials throughout the supply chain using blockchain technology can help to increase efficiency, reduce waste, and improve transparency.

There are also likely to be important implications for the future of work and the labor market. As automation and artificial intelligence become increasingly prevalent, many workers may find themselves displaced from traditional jobs. However, digital assets and blockchain technology offer new opportunities for entrepreneurship and innovation, and may help to create new jobs in emerging industries.

Overall, the rise of digital assets and blockchain technology represents an exciting and dynamic development in the world of business and economics. As these technologies continue to evolve and mature, they are likely to play an increasingly important role in shaping the future of these fields.

As we come to the end of this book, it is important to reflect on the implications of the topics covered for readers. Whether you are a business owner, entrepreneur, investor, student, or simply interested in the world of business, the information presented in this book can have significant implications for your career, personal life, and understanding of the world around you.

Firstly, the importance of innovation and entrepreneurship has been emphasized throughout the book. Innovation is essential for businesses to stay competitive and relevant in a rapidly changing world, while entrepreneurship is crucial for creating new businesses and driving economic growth. Readers can take away the importance of cultivating a culture of innovation within their organizations, and the value of taking calculated risks and embracing failure as a part of the entrepreneurial journey.

Secondly, the role of marketing and branding in business success has also been discussed. Effective marketing and branding can help businesses differentiate themselves from competitors and build a loyal customer base. Readers can learn the importance of developing a strong brand identity and using various marketing channels to reach their target audience.

Thirdly, the significance of finance and investment has been highlighted. Understanding financial management and investment strategies is essential for businesses to achieve long-term growth and success. Readers can learn about the different types of investments, such as stocks, bonds, and real estate, and the importance of diversification and risk management in their investment portfolios.

Fourthly, the impact of technology on society has been explored. Technology has revolutionized the way we live and work, and readers can gain insights into the potential benefits and challenges that technology can bring. The topics of digital assets and blockchain have been discussed in depth, highlighting their potential to disrupt traditional financial systems and provide new opportunities for investment and innovation.

Lastly, the importance of business ethics and social responsibility has been emphasized. Businesses have a responsibility to consider the impact of their actions on stakeholders and society as a whole. Readers can learn about the principles of ethical decision-making and the significance of whistleblowing, fair trade, and sustainability in business practices.

In conclusion, the implications of the topics covered in this book are vast and varied. Readers can take away insights into the importance of innovation, entrepreneurship, marketing and branding, finance and investment, technology and society, and business ethics. The information presented can help readers make informed decisions in their personal and professional lives, as well as gain a better understanding of the complex world of business and economics.

THE END

Glossary

Here are some key terms and definitions related to the topics covered in this book:

Economics: The study of how societies allocate resources to meet their needs and wants.

Finance: The study of how individuals and businesses manage their money, including investments, budgeting, and risk management.

Innovation: The process of creating new ideas, products, or services that provide value to customers.

Ethics: The principles and values that govern individual and organizational behavior, including honesty, integrity, and social responsibility.

Data analysis: The process of using statistical and analytical methods to interpret data and draw conclusions.

Macroeconomics: The study of the economy as a whole, including factors like inflation, unemployment, and gross domestic product.

Microeconomics: The study of individual consumer and producer behavior, including factors like supply and demand, market structures, and price elasticity.

Gross Domestic Product (GDP): The total value of goods and services produced within a country's borders in a given period of time.

Inflation: The rate at which the general level of prices for goods and services is increasing over time.

Unemployment: The percentage of the labor force that is not currently employed but is actively seeking work.

Business cycle: The fluctuation of economic activity over time, including periods of expansion and contraction.

Fiscal policy: Government policies related to taxation and spending that affect the economy.

Supply and demand: The relationship between the quantity of a good or service that producers are willing to offer and the quantity that consumers are willing to purchase at a given price.

Market structures: The characteristics of different types of markets, including competition, barriers to entry, and pricing power.

Consumer behavior: The study of how individuals make decisions about what goods and services to buy, and how much to buy.

Price elasticity: The degree to which the quantity of a good or service demanded changes in response to a change in its price.

Game theory: The study of strategic decision-making, including the behavior of individuals and firms in competitive situations.

Corporate finance: The study of how businesses manage their finances, including raising capital, making investments, and managing risk.

Investments: Assets purchased with the goal of generating income or appreciation, including stocks, bonds, and real estate.

Digital assets: Assets that exist in digital form, including cryptocurrencies and other blockchain-based assets.

Personal finance: The study of how individuals manage their finances, including budgeting, saving, and investing.

Financial ratios: Mathematical calculations used to evaluate the financial health of a business or investment.

Time value of money: The principle that a dollar received today is worth more than a dollar received in the future, due to the potential for earning interest or returns.

International trade: The exchange of goods and services between countries.

Tariffs and quotas: Taxes or limits on imports and exports, intended to protect domestic industries or regulate trade.

Exchange rates: The value of one currency in relation to another currency.

Balance of payments: The difference between a country's total exports and total imports of goods and services.

Comparative advantage: The ability of a country or business to produce a good or service at a lower opportunity cost than another country or business.

WTO: The World Trade Organization, an international organization that promotes free trade and settles disputes between member countries.

Public policy: Government policies and regulations that affect the economy and society.

Regulatory policy: A set of rules, guidelines, and principles established by a government or other regulatory body to oversee and control various economic activities and industries.

Monetary policy: Government policies related to the supply of money and credit in the economy, including interest rates and the money supply.

Regression analysis: a statistical method used to determine the relationship between one or more independent variables and a dependent variable

Stakeholder theory: a theory that suggests that a company should consider the interests of all stakeholders, including customers, employees, suppliers, and communities, rather than just its shareholders

Statistical analysis: the practice of collecting, analyzing, and interpreting data using statistical methods

Supply and demand: the relationship between the quantity of a product or service that producers are willing to supply and the quantity that consumers are willing to buy

Tax accounting: the practice of accounting for taxes, including calculating and preparing tax returns and minimizing tax liability

Time value of money: the concept that money today is worth more than the same amount of money in the future due to its earning potential

Unemployment: the state of being without work, but actively seeking employment

WTO (World Trade Organization): an international organization that promotes free trade by setting and enforcing rules and regulations for trade between its member countries.

Potential References

Introduction:

Mankiw, N. G. (2014). Principles of economics. Cengage Learning.

Chang, H.-J. (2014). Economics: The user's guide. Bloomsbury Press.

Stiglitz, J. E., Walsh, C. E., & Greenwald, B. C. (2014). Principles of macroeconomics. W. W. Norton & Company.

Chapter 1: Macroeconomics

Krugman, P. R., & Wells, R. (2014). Macroeconomics. Worth Publishers.

Blanchard, O. J. (2017). Macroeconomics. Pearson.

Mankiw, N. G. (2016). Macroeconomics. Macmillan.

Chapter 2: Microeconomics

Mankiw, N. G. (2014). Principles of microeconomics. Cengage Learning.

Varian, H. R. (2014). Intermediate microeconomics: A modern approach. WW Norton & Company.

Besanko, D., & Braeutigam, R. R. (2015). Microeconomics. Wiley.

Chapter 3: Finance

Brealey, R. A., Myers, S. C., & Allen, F. (2016). Principles of corporate finance. McGraw-Hill Education.

Bodie, Z., Kane, A., & Marcus, A. J. (2018). Essentials of investments. McGraw-Hill Education.

Gitman, L. J., Joehnk, M. D., & Smart, S. B. (2019). Fundamentals of investing. Pearson.

Chapter 4: International Trade

Krugman, P. R., Obstfeld, M., & Melitz, M. J. (2014). International economics: theory and policy. Pearson.

Appleyard, D. R., Field, A. J., & Cobb, S. L. (2018). International economics. McGraw-Hill Education.

Salvatore, D. (2017). International economics. John Wiley & Sons.

Chapter 5: Public Policy

Baumol, W. J., & Blinder, A. S. (2015). Economics: Principles and policy. Cengage Learning.

Stiglitz, J. E., & Walsh, C. E. (2015). Economics. W. W. Norton & Company.

Mankiw, N. G. (2015). Principles of economics. Cengage Learning.

Chapter 6: Accounting

Weygandt, J. J., Kimmel, P. D., & Kieso, D. E. (2019). Financial accounting: tools for business decision making. John Wiley & Sons.

Horngren, C. T., Sundem, G. L., Schatzberg, J. O., & Burgstahler, D. (2017). Introduction to management accounting. Pearson.

Warren, C. S., Reeve, J. M., & Duchac, J. (2016). Accounting. Cengage Learning.

Chapter 7: Business Ethics

Crane, A., & Matten, D. (2016). Business ethics: Managing corporate citizenship and sustainability in the age of globalization. Oxford University Press.

Carroll, A. B. (1991). The pyramid of corporate social responsibility: Toward the moral management of organizational stakeholders. Business Horizons, 34(4), 39-48.

Freeman, R. E., Harrison, J. S., Wicks, A. C., Parmar, B. L., & de Colle, S. (2010). Stakeholder theory: The state of the art. Cambridge University Press.

Chapter 8: Data Analysis

Gelman, A., & Hill, J. (2016). Data analysis using regression and multilevel/hierarchical models. Cambridge University Press.

Brynjolfsson, E., & McAfee, A. (2014). The second machine age: Work, progress, and prosperity in a time of brilliant technologies. W. W. Norton & Company.

Kshetri, N. (2018). Blockchain's roles in meeting key supply chain management objectives. International Journal of Information Management, 39, 80-89.

Chen, X., Ding, Y., & Xu, B. (2019). Prediction of bitcoin price based on blockchain transaction data. Journal of Intelligent & Fuzzy Systems, 36(1), 1-8.

Chapter 9: Case Studies

Healthcare:

Cutler, D. M., & Rosen, A. B. (2013). Understanding differences in health care spending between the United States and other high-income countries. JAMA, 309(10), 1014-1023.

Sood, N., & Huckfeldt, P. J. (2015). The potential for health care cost savings through use of blockchain technology. Harvard Business Review, 16(1), 1-5.

Technology, including blockchain and digital assets:

Narayanan, A., Bonneau, J., Felten, E., Miller, A., & Goldfeder, S. (2016). Bitcoin and Cryptocurrency Technologies: A Comprehensive Introduction. Princeton University Press.

Tapscott, D., & Tapscott, A. (2016). Blockchain revolution: how the technology behind bitcoin is changing money, business, and the world. Penguin.

Energy and environment:

Pachauri, R. K., Allen, M. R., Barros, V. R., Broome, J., Cramer, W., Christ, R., ... & Dubash, N. K. (2014). Climate change 2014: synthesis report. Contribution of Working Groups I, II and III to the fifth assessment report of the Intergovernmental Panel on Climate Change. IPCC.

Kaufman, G., & Younos, T. (2018). Blockchain technology in the energy sector: A systematic review of challenges and opportunities. Renewable and Sustainable Energy Reviews, 90, 536-550.

Education:

Reimers, F. M., & Schleicher, A. (2018). World Class: How to build a 21st-century school system. Strong Performers and Successful Reformers in Education Series. OECD Publishing.

Brynjolfsson, E., & McAfee, A. (2014). The second machine age: Work, progress, and prosperity in a time of brilliant technologies. WW Norton & Company.

International development:

Easterly, W. (2014). The tyranny of experts: Economists, dictators, and the forgotten rights of the poor. Basic Books.

Acemoglu, D., & Robinson, J. A. (2012). Why nations fail: the origins of power, prosperity, and poverty. Crown Business.

Conclusion:

Acemoglu, D., & Robinson, J. A. (2012). Why nations fail: the origins of power, prosperity, and poverty. Crown Business.

Brynjolfsson, E., & McAfee, A. (2014). The second machine age: Work, progress, and prosperity in a time of brilliant technologies. WW Norton & Company.

Tapscott, D., & Tapscott, A. (2016). Blockchain revolution: how the technology behind bitcoin is changing money, business, and the world. Penguin.

Implications for readers:

Stiglitz, J. E. (2019). People, power, and profits: Progressive capitalism for an age of discontent. WW Norton & Company.

Mazzucato, M. (2018). The value of everything: Making and taking in the global economy. PublicAffairs.

Thaler, R. H. (2015). Misbehaving: The making of behavioral economics. WW Norton & Company.